Traverse Theatre Company

Carthage Must Be Destroyed

by Alan Wilkins

cast in order of appearance

Marcus	Damian Lynch
Gregor	Sean Campion
David	Paul-James Corrigan
Cato	Tony Guilfoyle
Youth	Paul-James Corrigan

Director	Lorne Campbell
Designer	Kenny Miller
Lighting Designer	Renny Robertson
Composer	Philip Pinsky
Fight Director	Carter Ferguson
Voice & Dialect Coach	Ros Steen
Stage Manager	Lee Davis
Deputy Stage Manager	Gemma Smith
Assistant Stage Manager	Jenny Raith
Wardrobe Supervisor	Victoria Young
Wardrobe Assistant	Jane Gore

**First performed at the Traverse Theatre,
Friday 27 April 2007**

A Traverse Theatre Commission

THE TRAVERSE

Artistic Director Philip Howard

**A Rolls-Royce machine for promoting
new Scottish drama across Europe and beyond.**
(The Scotsman)

The Traverse's commissioning process embraces a spirit of innovation and risk-taking that has launched the careers of many of Scotland's best-known writers including John Byrne, David Greig, David Harrower and Liz Lochhead. It is unique in Scotland in that it fulfils the crucial role of providing the infrastructure, professional support and expertise to ensure the development of a dynamic theatre culture for Scotland.

**The importance of the Traverse is difficult
to overestimate . . . without the theatre, it is difficult
to imagine Scottish playwriting at all.** (Sunday Times)

From its conception in the 1960s, the Traverse has remained a pivotal venue during the Edinburgh Festival. It receives enormous critical and audience acclaim for its programming, as well as regularly winning awards. From 2001–05, Traverse Theatre productions of *Gagarin Way* by Gregory Burke, *Outlying Islands* by David Greig, *Iron* by Rona Munro, *The People Next Door* by Henry Adam, *Shimmer* by Linda McLean, *When the Bulbul Stopped Singing* by Raja Shehadeh and *East Coast Chicken Supper* by Martin J Taylor have won Fringe First or Herald Angel Awards (and occasionally both).

2006 was a record-breaking year for the Traverse as their Festival programme *Passion* picked up an incredible 14 awards including a Herald Angel Award for their own production of *Strawberries in January* by Evelyne de la Chenelière in a version by Rona Munro.

**The Traverse Theatre has established itself as
Scotland's leading exponent of new writing, with
a reputation that extends worldwide.** (The Scotsman)

The Traverse's success isn't limited to the Edinburgh stage, since 2001 Traverse productions of *Gagarin Way, Outlying Islands, Iron, The People Next Door, When the Bulbul Stopped Singing, The Slab Boys Trilogy, Mr Placebo* and *Helmet* have toured not only within Scotland and the UK, but in Sweden, Norway, the Balkans, Germany, USA, Iran, Jordan and Canada. This year, immediately following the 2006 festival, the Traverse's production of *Petrol Jesus Nightmare #5 (In the Time of the Messiah)* by Henry Adam was invited to perform at the International Festival in Priština, Kosovo and won the Jury Special Award for Production.

One of Europe's most important homes for new plays.
(Sunday Herald)

Now in its 14th year, the Traverse's annual Highlands & Islands tour is a crucial strand of their work. This commitment to Scottish touring has taken plays from their Edinburgh home to audiences all over Scotland. The Traverse has criss-crossed the nation performing at diverse locations from Shetland to Dumfries, Aberdeen to Benbecula. The Traverse's 2005 production *I was a Beautiful Day* was commissioned to open the new An Lanntair Arts Centre in Stornoway, Isle of Lewis.

Auld Reekie's most important theatre. (The Times)

The Traverse's work with young people is of supreme importance and takes the form of encouraging playwriting through its flagship education project *Class Act*, as well as the Young Writers' Group. *Class Act* is now in its 17th year and gives pupils the opportunity to develop their plays with professional playwrights and work with directors and actors to see the finished piece performed on stage at the Traverse. Last year, for the third year running, the project also took place in Russia. In 2004 *Articulate*, a large scale project based on the *Class Act* model, took place in West Dunbartonshire working with 11- to 14-year-olds. The hugely successful Young Writers' Group is open to new writers aged between 18 and 25 and the fortnightly meetings are led by a professional playwright.

The Traverse has an unrivalled reputation for producing contemporary theatre of the highest quality, invention and energy, and for its dedication to new writing. (Scotland on Sunday)

The Traverse is committed to working with international playwrights and, in 2005, produced *In the Bag* by Wang Xiaoli in a version by Ronan O'Donnell, the first-ever full production of a contemporary Chinese play in the UK. This project was part of the successful Playwrights in Partnership scheme, which unites international and Scottish writers, and brings the most dynamic new global voices to the Edinburgh stage. Other international Traverse partnerships have included work in Québec, Norway, Finland, France, Italy, Portugal and Japan.

www.traverse.co.uk

To find out about ways in which you can support the work of the Traverse please contact our Development Department
0131 228 3223 or development@traverse.co.uk

Charity No. SC002368

COMPANY BIOGRAPHIES

Lorne Campbell (Director)
Lorne trained at the Traverse Theatre on the Channel 4 Theatre Directors' Scheme from 2002–2004 and has been Associate Director since 2005. Other training: RSAMD (MDra) and Liverpool John Moores (BA Hons). Directing credits for the Traverse include the world premieres of *Distracted* by Morna Pearson, *White Point* by David Priestly, *Broke* by David Lescot in a version by Iain F MacLeod, *Melody* by Douglas Maxwell, *In the Bag* by Xiaoli Wang in a version by Ronan O'Donnell, *The Nest* by Alan Wilkins. Lorne was also Associate Director for *East Coast Chicken Supper* by Martin J Taylor and *The People Next Door* by Henry Adam (Balkan Tour 2004). Other theatre credits include: *Brokenville* (British Council/Young Audience's Ensemble of Togliatti) *The Dumb Waiter, Death and the Maiden, An Evening with Damon Runyon, A Comedy of Errors, As You Like It, Journey's End* (Forge Theatre); *The Chairs* (RSAMD); *The Cheviot, The Stag and the Black, Black Oil* (Taigh Chearsabhagh).

Sean Campion (*Gregor*)
Theatre credits include *Food* (The Imaginary Body, Edinburgh Fringe 2006); *Phaedra, The Cosmonaut's Last Message To The Woman He Once Loved In The Former Soviet Union* (Donmar Warehouse); *Blackwater Angel* (Finborough Theatre); *The Quare Fellow* (Oxford Stage Company); *Mayhem* (Royal Exchange Theatre, Manchester); *Beauty in a Broken Place, Good Evening Mr Collins, Hubert Murray's Widow* (Peacock Theatre); *Winners/Interior* (Young Vic Theatre); *Da, The Importance of Being Ernest, Observe the Sons of Ulster Marching Towards the Somme, Macbeth, The Silver Tassie, Big Maggie* (Abbey Theatre); *Stones in His Pockets* (Tour: West End, Broadway); *Waiting for Godot* (Lyric Theatre, Belfast), *The Mayor of Casterbridge* (Storytellers Theatre Company); *Northern Star* (Tinderbox Theatre Company); *Tarry Flynn, Mutabilitie* (Royal National Theatre); *Romeo and Juliet* (Riverbank Theatre), *Miss Julie* (Everyman Palace); *Equus, Canaries* (Gaiety Theatre). Television credits include *Holby City, EastEnders* (BBC); *Glenroe, Fair City, The Past* (RTE); *Echoes* (Channel 4). Film credits include *Timbuktu* (Yellow Asylum Films); *Goldfish Memory* (Goldfish Films).

Paul-James Corrigan (*David/Youth*)
Paul graduated from Coatbridge College in June 2004. Theatre credits include *Risk* (macrobert); *James and the Giant Peach, No Mean City, The Borrowers* (Citizens' Theatre); *Gobbo/Mancub*

(National Theatre of Scotland); *Free-Fall* (7:84 Theatre Company); *Mancub* (Vanishing Point/Soho Theatre). Television credits include *In Voluntary, Chewin' the Fat* (Comedy Unit/BBC Scotland).

Carter Ferguson (Fight Director)

Carter is an actor, director, fight director and designer working extensively in theatre, film and television. Recent fight directing credits include, for theatre, *Tutti Frutti, Mary Stuart, Home* (National Theatre of Scotland); *Ice Cream Dreams* (TAG Theatre Company/Citizens' Theatre); *Monks* (Royal Lyceum Theatre, Edinburgh); *The Bevellers, My Bloody Valentine, Shadow of a Gunman, No Mean City, Blood Wedding, Romeo and Juliet, Whatever Happened to Baby Jane?, Baby Doll, Cleo Camping Emmanuelle and Dick, Vernon God Little, Ruffian on the Stair* (Citizens' Theatre); *Yellow Moon* (TAG Theatre Company). Carter has also worked with Scottish Youth Theatre, Scottish Opera and Catherine Wheels Theatre Company. Fight directing credits for television include regular work on *River City* (BBC Scotland) and *Taggart* (SMG). As an actor Carter plays the recurring character Harry Black in *River City* (BBC Scotland).

Tony Guilfoyle (*Cato*)

Theatre credits include *Woyzeck* (The Gate/St Anne's Warehouse, New York); for the LePage Company *The Dragon's Trilogy* (Barbican/International Tour); *Geometry of Miracles* (Royal National Theatre/International Tour); *Kinder/Leider* (Lincoln Centre, New York). Other theatre credits include *Shadowmouth* (Sheffield Crucible); *The Iceman Cometh, The LA Plays* (Almeida Theatre); *Shopping and Fucking, Same Old Moon* (Gielgud Theatre/Queens International Tour); *Same Old Moon* (Gielgud Theatre); *Outskirts* (RSC); *The Queen and I* (Out of Joint); *San Diego* (Edinburgh International Festival/Tron Theatre); *Teorama* (Queen Elizabeth Hall/Opera Della, Roma); *Imitations of Life, The Supermale, Loving Reno* (Bush Theatre); *Awakenings* (Riverside Studios); *Uses of Enchantment* (The Place); *L'Ascensore*, (ICA); *Translations,Says I Says He* (Bristol Old Vic); *Dealer's Choice* (Theatre Clwyd); *A Flea in Her Ear* (West Yorkshire Playhouse). Television credits include *Rome* (HBO); *Bleak House, The Virgin Queen* (BBC); *Father Ted* (Hat Trick Productions); *The Murder of Stephen Lawrence, Breed of Heroes* (Granada); *Murder City* (Talkback Thames). Film credits include *The Return* (FilmFour); *Death Row* (Team Worx); *Missing It* (Channel 4).

Damian Lynch (*Marcus*)

Damian trained at the Webber Douglas Academy in London. Theatre credits include *School for Scandal* (Salisbury Playhouse); *If It Be Not*

Good, The Devil Is In It (Shakespeare's Globe); Robinson Crusoe (Theatre Royal, Winchester); Black Diamonds (Quondam Theatre, National Tour); Dirty Butterfly (Cockpit Theatre, London) and Duke of Ephesus in Comedy of Errors (Cliveden). Television credits include The Bill (Talkback Thames); Little Britain, Casualty, Waking the Dead, Judge John Deed (BBC). Film credits include Munich (Dreamworks). Damian has worked extensively on radio, appearing in over 60 radio productions including Ouagadougou (BBC Radio 3 Africa Season), Arthur, Flash for Freedom (BBC Radio 4). Recent productions have included She, Small Island, Madame Butterfly's Child, The Resistible Rise of Arturo Ui and Metropolis (all for BBC Radio 4 and BBC World Service Drama). Damian was the winner of the BBC Carleton Hobbs Radio Award 2003 and was recently a member of the BBC Radio Drama Company 2006. Recent audio book narrations include the autobiography of Johnson Beharry V.C, Barefoot Soldier: A Tale of Extreme Valour. Damian also works regularly as a voiceover artist.

Kenny Miller (Designer)

Kenny is a freelance director and designer who was, until recently, Head of Design and Associate Director at the Citizens' Theatre. He has worked extensively in theatre for many years for companies such as the RSC, Barbican, Mark Taper Forum, Shared Experience Theatre Company, Greenwich Theatre, Scottish Opera, Newcastle Opera House, Tron Theatre and Toronto International Festival. Current projects include Koanga, an opera by Delius at Sadler's Wells to mark the anniversary of the abolition of slavery, designs for His Dark Materials by Philip Pullman for Scottish Youth Theatre, his own adaptation of the Louise Welsh novel Tamburlaine Must Die, which he will also direct, and a new version of Jack and the Beanstalk by Jonathan Harvey at the Barbican Theatre.

Philip Pinsky (Composer)

Philip was a founder member of electro-acoustic group Finitribe, releasing five albums and performing over a period of 15 years. He now composes for film, theatre, TV and radio. In theatre he has composed scores for Roam (Grid Iron/NTS); The Merchant of Venice, Faust 1 and 2 (Royal Lyceum Theatre, Edinburgh); Fierce, The Houghmagandie Pack, Fermentation, Decky Does A Bronco (Grid Iron); Variety (Edinburgh International Festival/Grid Iron); A Chaste Maid in Cheapside, The Whizzkid, Ghost Ward (Almeida Theatre); DeoxyriboNucleic Acid (Lyceum Youth Theatre/NT Connections); Oedipus (NTS Young Company); The Man Who Was Thursday (Red

Shift Theatre Company). He was winner of the Critics Award for Theatre in Scotland 2005 for best use of music in theatre. Other work includes *Extraneous Noises Off* (BBC Radio 3, winner of Sony Radio Award); *Art and Soul* (BBC Scotland); *Ninewells, Harley Street* (BBC1); education projects for the Scottish Chamber Orchestra and the signature music for MTV's European mobile phone channel. Future work includes *Once Upon a Dragon* (Grid Iron/Children's International Theatre Festival).

Renny Robertson (Lighting Designer)
Renny is Chief Electrician at the Traverse Theatre. Previous lighting design for the Traverse includes *Heritage, Homers, Chic Nerds, The Trestle at Pope Lick Creek* and *Lazybed*. He has also relit Traverse Productions on tour to Canada, Germany and Hungary. Renny has worked and toured with several other theatre companies including Plan B and Lung Ha's. He also toured with The Proclaimers.

Ros Steen (Voice & Dialect Coach)
Ros trained at RSAMD and has worked extensively in theatre, film and TV. For the Traverse: *strangers, babies,* the *Tilt* triple bill, *Gorgeous Avatar, Melody, I was a Beautiful Day, East Coast Chicken Supper, The Found Man, In the Bag, Shimmer, The Nest, The Slab Boys Trilogy, Dark Earth, Homers, Outlying Islands, The Ballad of Crazy Paola, The Trestle at Pope Lick Creek, Heritage* (2001 and 1998), *Among Unbroken Hearts, Shetland Saga, Solemn Mass for a Full Moon in Summer* (as co-director), *King of the Fields, Highland Shorts, Family, Kill the Old Torture Their Young, Chic Nerds, Greta, Lazybed, Knives in Hens, Passing Places, Bondagers, Road to Nirvana, Sharp Shorts, Marisol, Grace in America*. Recent theatre credits include *The Bevellers, Shadow of a Gunman, No Mean City, Whatever Happened to Baby Jane?, Mystery of the Rose Bouquet* (Citizens' Theatre); *Sweet Bird of Youth, The Talented Mr Ripley, The Graduate, A Lie of the Mind* (Dundee Rep); *Black Watch, Mancub, Miss Julie* (National Theatre of Scotland); *The Wonderful World of Dissocia* (Edinburgh International Festival/Drum Theatre Plymouth/Tron Theatre), *The Rise and Fall of Little Voice* (Visible Fictions); *Perfect Pie* (Stellar Quines); *The Small Things* (Paines Plough); *My Mother Said I Never Should* (West Yorkshire Playhouse). Film credits include *Greyfriars Bobby* (Piccadilly Pictures); *Gregory's Two Girls* (Channel Four Films). Television credits include *Sea of Souls, Rockface, Two Thousand Acres of Sky, Monarch of the Glen, Hamish Macbeth* (BBC).

Alan Wilkins (Writer)

Alan was brought up in Edinburgh and, after time spent in Glasgow, Poznan and Madrid, returned to the city in 1998. Since then he has worked as a drama teacher (1998–2004) and as a full-time writer and theatre practitioner (2004–present). His first Traverse Theatre commission, *The Nest*, was produced at the Traverse and then toured the Highlands & Islands in 2004. Alan is also playwright-mentor for the Traverse Theatre's Young Writers' Group and represented Scotland as a tutor playwright at the 2006 Interplay festival in Lichtenstein. In the last two years he has worked as a writer/actor/collaborator on projects for ek productions, Dundee Rep Theatre, City Moves and Aldeburgh Festival, and is currently a playwright tutor for the MA Theatre Studies course at Glasgow University. *Carthage Must Be Destroyed* is his second Traverse commission.

The Traverse would like to thank the members of the Development Board:

Adrienne Sinclair Chalmers, Stephen Cotton, Roddy Martine, Paddy Scott and Teri Wishart

The Traverse Theatre receives financial assistance from:

The Binks Trust, The Barcapel Foundation, The Calouste Gulbenkian Foundation, The Canadian High Commission, The Craignish Trust, The Cross Trust, The Cruden Foundation, Gouvernement de Québec, James Thom Howat Charitable Trust, The Japan Foundation, The Lloyds TSB Foundation for Scotland, The Peggy Ramsay Foundation, Ronald Duncan Literary Foundation, Sky Youth Action Fund, Tay Charitable Trust, The Thistle Trust

For their continued generous support of Traverse productions, the Traverse thanks:

Habitat; Marks and Spencer, Princes Street; Camerabase

Charity No. SC002368

SPONSORSHIP AND DEVELOPMENT

We would like to thank the following
corporate funders for their support

LUMISON HBJ Gateley Wareing

To find out how you can benefit
from being a Traverse Corporate Funder,
please contact our Development Department
on 0131 228 3223 / development@traverse.co.uk

**The Traverse Theatre's work
would not be possible without the support of**

ARE YOU DEVOTED?

Our Devotees are:

Stewart Binnie, Katie Bradford, Adrienne Sinclair Chalmers, Adam Fowler, Anne Gallacher, Keith Guy, Helen Pitkethly, Michael Ridings

The Traverse could not function without the generous support of our patrons. In March 2006 the Traverse Devotees was launched to offer a whole host of exclusive benefits to our loyal supporters.

Become a Traverse Devotee for £28 per month or £350 per annum and receive:

- A night at the theatre including six tickets, drinks and a backstage tour

- Your name inscribed on a brick in our wall

- Sponsorship of one of our brand new Traverse 2 seats

- Invitations to Devotees' events

- Your name featured on this page in Traverse Theatre Company scripts and a copy mailed to you

- Free hire of the Traverse Bar Café (subject to availability)

Bricks in our wall and seats in Traverse 2 are also available separately. Inscribed with a message of your choice, these make ideal and unusual gifts.

To join the Devotees or to discuss giving us your support in another way, please contact our Development Department on 0131 228 3223 / development@traverse.co.uk

TRAVERSE THEATRE – THE COMPANY

CARTHAGE MUST BE DESTROYED

Alan Wilkins

For Robbie Wilkins

Therefore, my Harry,
Be it thy course to busy giddy minds
With foreign quarrels; that action, hence borne out,
May waste the memory of the former days.

Shakespeare, *Henry IV Part II*, Act IV, Scene 2

All wars are different. All wars are the same.

Jarhead (screenplay by William Broyles Jr.,
book by Anthony Swofford)

Characters

CATO, *consul, late fifties*

GREGOR, *senator, forties*

MARCUS, *up-and-coming politician, twenties*

DAVID, *Cato's nephew, sixteen*

YOUTH, *Carthaginian, sixteen*

This text went to press before the end of rehearsals so may differ slightly from the play as performed.

ACT ONE

Rome, 149 BC

Scene One

A sunken bath. Upstage are steps leading up to a seating area.
GREGOR *is in the bath.* MARCUS *enters, strips and also gets into the bath.*

MARCUS. That's not too bad.

GREGOR. What's not too bad?

MARCUS. The temperature. Not too hot, not too cold.

GREGOR. It's perfect.

MARCUS. Well . . .

GREGOR. The temperature's important to me. I employ good people to make sure it's perfect. 'Not too bad' doesn't cover it. 'Perfect' does.

MARCUS. Yes . . . I see. It is very good. Have you been here long?

GREGOR. Half an hour. Where have you been?

MARCUS. I was waiting outside. I didn't know if I was supposed to go in. If that was the arrangement. Then I worried Cato was early . . . he'd gone in already. He'd think I was late.

GREGOR. So you panicked. Well, you're here now. Relax. Enjoy it. You know what Cato's like – 'Let's meet at the bath', very civilised. But when he gets here it'll be business, business, business. I wanted a proper bath. (*Pause.*) I got my last commission at the amphitheatre. I'd sponsored a chariot, and he's going on about taxation. 'Let's have a meeting,' I said. 'A meeting about taxation. But let me watch my chariot.'

MARCUS. You didn't say that.

GREGOR. I did.

MARCUS. Right.

GREGOR. But there's no talking to him at the moment.

MARCUS. He listens to me.

GREGOR. Bollocks.

MARCUS. He does. Last time we met he told me. 'I value your input,' he said.

GREGOR. Meaningless.

MARCUS. He didn't have to say it. He was pretty curt with some of the others. You know Julian?

GREGOR. Which one?

MARCUS. From the south. Big drinker.

GREGOR. I know of him.

MARCUS. Cato threw him out. Said it cost a lot of money to finance these fact-finding trips, and he expected a damn sight more than anecdote. That's why he liked my approach. Hard facts. People counted, tax discrepancies noted, resources and weaponry clearly listed. He nodded. Smiled. 'I value your input.'

GREGOR. He's a fool, then. Anecdotal evidence is great. Very difficult to disprove.

MARCUS. You wouldn't call him a fool to his face.

GREGOR. Probably not. But I would disagree with him. You're playing the wrong game, sticking with Cato come what may. There's a lot of people criticising him at the moment.

MARCUS. Who?

GREGOR. Oh, nobody's going public. Just now, it's a whisper. But whispers get louder. Sooner or later he's going to have to get rough or step aside.

MARCUS. And you'll take over . . .

GREGOR. Wouldn't touch the job. I like the fine things in life – wine, good food, a young lad. These days you're expected to work all day in the top jobs. I'm happy where I am. Just the right amount of influence. People respect you, but deep down they don't really think you can change anything. So you sort out the odd tax problem for someone and accept their gratitude. It's a good game to be in. You should try it.

MARCUS. I am trying. But it's not easy.

GREGOR. Hmm. Background's still important.

MARCUS. I know.

GREGOR. But there have been others. African senators, I mean.

MARCUS. I'm not African.

GREGOR. Well . . . not technically, I suppose.

MARCUS. I've never been to Africa.

GREGOR. Really?

MARCUS. My father and mother have never been to Africa.

GREGOR. I thought your father was a slave.

MARCUS. My grandfather was a slave.

GREGOR. Might help. Now's not the time, but somewhere down the line it might suit someone to give you a lift up. Ex-slave family in the Senate – it's a good human-interest story. Just don't put all your eggs in Cato's basket.

MARCUS. I don't want to get to the Senate on the back of a human-interest story. I want to get there on merit. On a platform of sustained public service. Cato's in charge at the moment, so serving the public means serving him. If somebody else takes over, I'll serve them.

GREGOR. Not a bad defence if things go belly-up.

MARCUS. There's no reason why things can't carry on as they are.

GREGOR. People aren't happy.

MARCUS. People don't know how lucky they are.

A youth walks in, naked.

GREGOR. Bloody hell. Who the fuck is that?

MARCUS. I don't know.

GREGOR. Absolutely beautiful.

MARCUS. Don't be obscene.

GREGOR. What a glorious specimen.

MARCUS. You disgust me.

GREGOR. Oh, don't be so wet. Admire. The muscle definition, the noble bearing. The face, the chest, the legs . . . Ah, youth . . . It really does nothing for you?

MARCUS. I think it's degenerate. It's not what I would call a Roman activity.

GREGOR. Well, it should be. Hanging around the baths, looking at boys – it's the perfect morning.

MARCUS. Cato's late.

GREGOR. Cato's the leader – he can't be late. We're just early. (*Looking at the youth.*) Have you seen him before? He's from a wealthy family. I'll have to find out who his father is – tread carefully.

MARCUS. How do you know he's from a wealthy family?

GREGOR. A sense. The smell of him. Breathtaking. He's just too much my type – probably already got a sponsor.

MARCUS. A sponsor. That's what they call it now.

GREGOR. Stop being cynical. I could be of great use to a young man making his way in the world, whoever his father is.

MARCUS. He can probably hear you.

GREGOR. I hope so. I certainly wasn't saying it for your sake. And I haven't got long. Cato'll have him thrown out when he arrives. (*To the youth.*) Hello there. Don't be unsociable. Join us.

The youth, DAVID, *does so.*

DAVID. I didn't want to disturb you.

GREGOR. Not at all. We were just talking about sport. It's not often us old fellows get the chance to talk to the young. I welcome the opportunity to be energised by the dynamism and optimism of your vision.

DAVID. What vision?

MARCUS. My friend Gregor is fond of the company of the young.

GREGOR. Fond . . . that's about right.

DAVID. I don't have a vision.

GREGOR. What . . . nothing at all?

DAVID. Nothing. Not a vision, anyway.

GREGOR. How wonderful. Perhaps this . . . bleakness, this dark refusal to compromise your present by admitting the future . . . perhaps that is your vision.

MARCUS. Pathetic. You don't believe that for a moment.

GREGOR. I'm trying to understand our young friend.

MARCUS (*to* DAVID). Tell me, when you look at the country – as a whole – is there really nothing you'd like to change?

DAVID. Why would I spend time worrying about that? It is what it is. I can't do anything.

GREGOR. I don't know if that makes you impossibly old or impossibly young.

MARCUS. Certainly it's a bit short on – what was it – dynamism and optimism.

GREGOR. But still . . . but still. What do you enjoy in life? What punctures that cynical shell and allows the rest of us to see you smile?

DAVID. I like poetry.

GREGOR. Excellent. If a little confusing. I know many poets and shall make it my obligation to introduce you to some of our finest. They all have probably a little too much vision, so some kind of mutual influence should be healthy for all of you.

DAVID. I'm not that keen on other people's stuff. I just like writing it. I don't really need any help. Thank you, though.

GREGOR. We all need a little help from time to time. You have an income, I suppose?

DAVID. I'm still living at home. And I'm about to start working for my uncle – as a secretary.

MARCUS. It seems as if your . . . charity . . . really isn't needed on this occasion.

GREGOR. I will content myself with having made a generous offer which I will repeat whenever bidden. For now, though, it seems there is nothing to be done for you, and your contribution in any kind of exchange of views is clearly limited. Please now, leave us to converse of adult matters.

DAVID. I'm to go?

GREGOR. Yes. Feel free to enjoy your own company in a far corner, but the time for chatting has gone. We have business to attend to.

DAVID (*shrugs*). OK.

He removes himself to a far corner of the bath. GREGOR follows him with his eyes.

GREGOR. A shame.

MARCUS. I've never seen you in action before.

GREGOR. No?

MARCUS. I've heard the stories, but I've never seen it. I had no idea you were quite so . . . obvious. It's revolting.

GREGOR. It's harmless banter in the baths. Nothing at all. An offer of altruistic intent towards the next generation of Rome was spurned by its intended beneficiary. End of story. No threats or bullying, no abuse of power. If this becomes part of the gossip about me, I shall know who to blame.

MARCUS. Don't take it out on me.

GREGOR. Well, you could have done the decent thing. Left for a while.

MARCUS. We're meeting Cato. I'm not going to be late just so that you can fail in a less embarrassing way.

GREGOR. Where is the old cunt?

MARCUS. Gregor!

GREGOR. I say it at least with a little affection.

MARCUS. If he finds out . . .

GREGOR. You're far too timid. You don't get to be number one around here without being a bit of a cunt, to put it mildly. Some call him a cunt with admiration, some with vitriol. It's his job to know the difference.

MARCUS. It's his job to look after the Republic.

GREGOR. That's not the way he sees it. Cato's a pragmatist. That's how he got to the top and it's how he intends to stay there. Luckily for Rome it suits Cato to see its people happy. But at some point he'll be gone. It's up to the rest of us to identify when that point's about to be reached and either replace him, gain more power under a new man or at least stay where we are. Not losing status – that's the key.

MARCUS. You have no sense of civic duty at all, do you?

GREGOR. Of course . . . It's just not as developed as my sense of self-preservation. I have certain appetites . . . things that give me pleasure, so I work to afford them. My family life is tolerable – I like my wife, and the children aren't around much. Being a senator allows this. If I help a few people on the way – excellent.

MARCUS. You've certainly helped me.

GREGOR. Thank you.

MARCUS. You're the reason I want to be a senator.

GREGOR. I hope this isn't going to be disrespectful.

MARCUS. I'll say no more. You're the reason I want to be a senator.

GREGOR. I value your input. (*Silence*.) When you want to stab someone in the back it's never a good idea to tell them in advance. Unless you're planning something very clever. In your position you need allies, not friends. When you realise the difference you can sit at the big boys' table.

CATO *enters*. GREGOR *and* MARCUS *stand up*.

GREGOR *and* MARCUS. Cato.

CATO. Please, sit down. (*Enters the bath.*) Sorry I kept you waiting.

GREGOR. No problem.

MARCUS. I've only just got here.

CATO. But I've only just arrived.

MARCUS. Yes . . .

CATO. I'm at least twenty minutes late.

GREGOR. Nearer half an hour.

CATO. I always intend to be ten minutes late, so it's only twenty. But yes – I take your point. Technically I'm half an hour late. And you've just arrived. Which means you're what . . . twenty, twenty-five minutes late for the first meeting I've ever scheduled with you. Which I find staggering.

MARCUS. I . . . I don't know what to say.

CATO. There seem to be two possibilities. One is that you were, in fact, on time and lied as a social pleasantry to make me feel better about my own timekeeping. The second is that you are either insolent or inept, neither of which would make it worthwhile continuing this meeting.

MARCUS. It's the first. The first one you said. I was here early. Ask Gregor.

CATO. No need. You being insolent or inept would have represented a serious error of judgement on my part. I knew you were here on time.

MARCUS. Sorry. I wasn't thinking.

CATO. Don't lie to make me feel better about things. That's what far too many are doing. I need you for the opposite. Your honest opinions. Tactfully expressed, but what you think.

MARCUS. I'm at your service.

GREGOR. Doesn't sound like my strong point, Cato. You sure you want me?

CATO. I'm sure.

GREGOR. There's a lad in the corner. I'll get him to leave.

CATO *looks around, claps his hands.*

CATO. Come here, lad.

DAVID *comes over, smiling.*

DAVID. Yes, Uncle.

CATO. David, I want you to meet a couple of people you're going to be working with.

DAVID. We've met.

CATO. When?

DAVID. Earlier. They sent me away. He sent me away.

CATO. He offered you favours?

DAVID. I don't know. I think so. It was quite a mixed message.

CATO. There's to be none of that. Understand?

GREGOR. I was being friendly.

CATO. None of it. Are we clear?

GREGOR. Perfectly.

CATO. He's my nephew. My brother's son. He's off-limits.

GREGOR. It was idle chat.

CATO. I'd like to cut your balls off.

DAVID. There was no harm done.

CATO. It disgusts me. The whole business is draining us. Morally. People should stop and the example should come from the top.

GREGOR. Do you want me to leave? Because I'm not that arsed about staying if you're just going to bang on about moral purity.

CATO. How dare you speak to me like that!

GREGOR. Look, he's the sycophant. We've established that.
I've no idea what my role is, but it's not going to be putting
up with this shit. Nothing happened. I sent him away. Let's
get on with it.

Pause. CATO *laughs.*

CATO. Gregor, you've not changed. That's what I like about
you. You don't like taking shit. You understand the game,
though perhaps you play it for the wrong reasons. No matter
. . . I'd like to cut your balls off, but for now I'll settle for
having you on my side. You help me, you help Rome, and
you help yourself.

GREGOR. I am on your side. It's the only side to be on.

CATO. We both know that's not true. And I know you'll be
keeping your options open, so let's make this easy. I don't
need to know any names. You don't need to mention any
specific details. I just need an overview. A general description.
What is the extent of the hostility against me?

GREGOR. You're asking the wrong person.

CATO. I'm not suggesting you're involved. There's not a hint
of accusation. But even your friends say that you're . . .
very sociable. You receive a lot of invitations and you tend
to accept.

GREGOR. What else do these friends say about me?

CATO. That you're not ambitious. You're fairly content with
what you've got. I assume that refers to power. Wealth, I'm
thinking, may be a different matter.

GREGOR. Are you trying to buy me?

MARCUS. Maybe it's sponsorship.

CATO *looks at him. No need for words* – MARCUS *is to
shut up.*

GREGOR. Money's important. Anyone who says it isn't has
too much of the stuff. But it's never been the reason I get
out of bed in the morning. It's a bit tight for everyone at the
moment. One copes.

CATO. Trust me – there'll be money to pass around soon
enough. To the right people.

GREGOR. It's a policy of mine not to trust people who say
'Trust me' – but if you're not looking for names, and you're
not going to blame the messenger, then why not? Let's talk.

CATO. Thank you.

DAVID. Should I take notes?

CATO. Absolutely not. It's always better just to remember this
sort of thing. We may write some of it up later, we may not.
As a rule, note-taking is an unnecessary risk. But pay
attention.

GREGOR. What do you mean, you might write some of it up
later? This is off the record or it's not happening.

CATO. Of course it's off the record. Any notes will reflect that.

GREGOR. I'm not sure I understand the need for a secretary.

CATO. It's . . . a more general apprenticeship. David here has
a keen mind.

GREGOR (*shrugs*). What do you want to know?

CATO. Like I said, the level of hostility. Is it a . . . a passing
shower, or something more persistent?

GREGOR. Some say you've lost your grip on things. There's
no ambition, no vitality. We should be rolling in it, but
people are having to cut back.

CATO. I see.

GREGOR. Others say you've got no sense of priorities. That
you rail and hector us about moral degeneracy because it's
easier than fixing the economy. That you're more interested
in image than substance. That you interfere when it's not
needed, and do nothing when something needs to be done.
That you have opinions but no strategy; you listen only to a
small band of favourites; you've lost authority; you don't
understand complex issues; your rhetoric lacks conviction;
your health is suspect and your intellect on the wane. Some
say that sometimes – no, often – you allow your wife to
make policy.

CATO. Lies.

GREGOR. I argue with these people, I really do. But to little effect, I'm afraid.

MARCUS. You should report them.

GREGOR. For what? Opinions?

MARCUS. We should know who they are.

GREGOR. Not at all. Why force people into a position? It hardens their argument. These whispers multiply easily enough without any help. Most people who talk of politics are fools. Win them back.

CATO. Nephew. In your circles, do they say such things?

DAVID. My friends know who my uncle is. They say nothing.

CATO. You're being honest? I need honesty – at the moment.

DAVID. I'm being honest.

CATO. Good. The chattering classes are poisoning the air, but so far it's contained.

DAVID. Though sometimes . . .

CATO. Yes?

DAVID. Sometimes I find myself wondering if their silence is, in fact, a tactful rebuke. Two years ago they were always asking about you.

CATO. I see.

GREGOR. There's no . . . there's no alternative. That's in your favour. The disillusionment isn't just about you. It's widespread. Especially amongst the young.

DAVID. I think that's true.

MARCUS. Taxes are hurting.

CATO. The taxes are being used almost entirely for the benefit of the people. Why are people yearning for a time when we took what we wanted from them and built ourselves holiday homes with the proceeds?

GREGOR. We were a richer country. Everyone had more. People don't have a problem with corruption, they have a problem with hunger.

CATO. These are the same people who a few years ago would pay more money for a jar of smoked fish than for an ox-driver. And now the bastards complain . . . Well, we'll give them what they want.

MARCUS. Money?

CATO. Money. And leadership. We'll make Rome rich again and they'll know who did it.

GREGOR. A good plan. Might need a bit of fleshing out in the details department.

MARCUS. I've been spending a lot of time looking at taxation. I could come up with a paper. A set of proposals. I believe that with a new approach, cutting down the amount we take directly from the populus but increasing targeted levies, we could increase the take by up to ten per cent. And we look like the good guys.

CATO. Write that paper. David: there's a lesson there. Young men who want to get on – they put in the work. Always thinking. Well done. But it's a plan for prosperity. We need to create more money before we can take it away. Gregor?

GREGOR. Yes?

CATO. Any thoughts?

GREGOR. Plenty of thoughts.

CATO. Any relevant thoughts?

GREGOR. No.

CATO. No?

GREGOR. Nothing. I'm not even trying.

CATO. I see.

GREGOR. You have a plan. I think I know what it is.

CATO. I suspect you don't.

GREGOR. Bloody hell, Cato. You're going to go after Carthage.

CATO. How the . . . ?

GREGOR. It's obvious.

CATO. I haven't discussed it with anyone.

GREGOR. Yes, you have. And you've had encouraging words.
You see, Marcus, there's an order to things. You should be
flattered that Cato wants to meet you in a bath, but don't
believe you're the first on the list. By the time the likes of
you and me are involved, the decision's been made.

CATO. Not quite. I'm here personally. If we'd made a decision
you'd hear about it like everybody else.

MARCUS. But it is Carthage?

CATO. Yes. And we have made a . . . not a decision, but . . .

MARCUS. A timetable towards a decision.

CATO. Yes.

MARCUS. A resolution.

CATO. No, not a resolution. That comes much later. Books
need to be balanced first. We have some money put aside,
but it is going to cost people. Belts will have to be
tightened.

MARCUS. Of course. (*To* GREGOR.) You'd already heard
this?

GREGOR. Not much. A flutter of a rumour.

CATO. If Gregor's only heard a little, it's fairly secure. Which
is the way we wanted it. Until now.

MARCUS. I don't understand. Carthage isn't a threat.

GREGOR. Yes, it is.

CATO. You think so?

GREGOR. You've decided it is. That's the point. And people
won't accept a bit of short-term poverty unless it's seen to be.

CATO. Frugality, not poverty. If people focus on what they
need for once, not what they desire, there'll be no problems.

MARCUS. We beat them last time.

CATO. We were too generous. We let them rebuild.

MARCUS. But are they a threat? I haven't heard anything.

CATO. David, before today, have you heard anyone say that
    Carthage is a threat?

DAVID. No.

CATO. But now, since you came here, have you?

DAVID. Yes.

CATO. So if anyone were to ask you the question, do you
    consider Carthage to be a threat to the security and well-
    being of the Roman Republic, what would you answer?

DAVID. I would answer that sources at the highest level lead
    me to believe that, yes, Carthage represents a clear danger
    to us.

CATO. Marcus, the youth have heard of this – I can't believe
    you're so poorly connected.

GREGOR. I understand part of this, Cato. But only part.

CATO. Which is unusual, for so shrewd a mind.

GREGOR. Drum up a bit of an overseas hoo-hah, take
    people's mind off things back here. It's worked before,
    might work again. And you're taking on someone we
    should beat, which is a good move . . .

CATO. I need to stop you. I'm aware this is an informal
    meeting. I'm aware too of the charge some will level at me.

GREGOR. Of political opportunism.

CATO. Some will call it that.

GREGOR. Of sacrificing lives to win a popularity contest.

CATO. Don't go too far.

GREGOR. This is what they'll say.

CATO. Perhaps. Which is why, informal or not, I will never
    refer to this plan as an overseas hoo-hah. Gentlemen, the
    truth starts today. The truth is that Carthage is a threat. That
    does not change.

MARCUS. Right. Carthage is a threat.

GREGOR. Fine. But how does prosecuting a war against a country we've already plundered help our economy?

CATO. That was fifty years ago. They've done well since then, believe me.

GREGOR. 'Believe me, trust me' . . . I'm breaking a lot of my own rules here.

CATO. Very well. Don't believe me. Don't trust me. I don't need you to do either. All I require of you is that you do as you're fucking told. Carthage must be destroyed, but it starts with a whisper. In the baths, in the street . . . the usual Gregor magic, get the ball rolling. I need you to start this off. Marcus, your strength is strategy. As soon as you hear any talk of this, start lobbying for a role in it. David, you're the runner. Arrange regular meetings and report back to me. When we're up and running, the three of you are my eyes and ears on this.

DAVID. Of course.

CATO. One-to-one meetings with Gregor in the bath are not to be permitted.

GREGOR. For fuck's sake.

CATO (*getting up to leave*). My decision has to be a response. A response to the growing clamour of voices urging me to take action. I want to hear that clamour soon. Get to work. Thank you for your time.

Lights down.

Scene Two

GREGOR *is standing, clothed, by the bath.* DAVID *hovers by the entrance.*

GREGOR. Well, come in.

DAVID. My uncle . . .

GREGOR. Your uncle is a fine man. I won't have a word said against him. Any of my regulars – even in joke – if they say anything about him at all that could be construed as disrespectful . . . that's it. They're dead to me. I don't want their custom. Privately though, if he has a fault, and it's not really a fault, it's more a . . . a characteristic . . . a trait of personality that could be viewed as negative. And if he has such a characteristic, it's that, for whatever reasons, he is a deeply suspicious man. Often wrongly so.

DAVID. Even so . . . he did give an order.

GREGOR. Or was it just a guideline, I wonder . . . ? Curtly reminding me of certain boundaries that of course must be observed. It's obviously important to remain true to the spirit of that injunction. But the specifics . . . what was the instruction again?

DAVID. No one-to-one meetings with you in the bath.

GREGOR. Good, good. We remember it the same. In the bath. Not in the bath house, not by the bath, but specifically in the bath. We're on safe ground here. Enter, please.

DAVID *does so*.

Well, embrace me.

DAVID. Embrace you?

GREGOR. A brief hand-to-shoulder contact. A standard social interaction kick-starting a conversation between adults. It should be done as quickly and naturally as possible.

DAVID *approaches*.

Right, place your left hand on my right shoulder and your right hand on my left shoulder.

DAVID *does so*.

You say my name – confidently, lightly. My first name.

DAVID. Gregor.

GREGOR. David. Then we break.

They do so.

Always embrace.

DAVID. What are we doing here?

GREGOR. I want to show you something. Come.

He guides DAVID *to a pillar, where there are some graffiti.*

DAVID. 'Fuck Carthage.'

GREGOR. There's some in the back room as well, 'Carthage scum are going to hell', but I'm not taking you through there.

DAVID. Why not?

GREGOR. The back room has a reputation. Undeserved, but there you are.

DAVID. Grafitti. It's a good idea. I should have thought about it. But I think Cato wanted more in a week than you scribbling on a few pillars. He has you down as a networker.

GREGOR. And he's right. When I put my mind to a project, I surprise myself. I didn't write this. I've no idea who did. That's what makes it so beautiful.

DAVID. I see what you mean.

GREGOR. It's become a talking point. There's still widespread opposition at the moment, but at least it's an issue.

DAVID. Word has it that you're part of that opposition. When you give your opinion, you're against the war. Cato's none too happy. I told him you must be working to a plan. I assume that's the case.

Pause.

GREGOR. Did you know I owned this?

DAVID. I thought you owned part of it.

GREGOR. The others are just names on paper. Essentially it's mine. I've four of them, plus my estate and some other bits and pieces.

DAVID. Politics has been good to you.

GREGOR. No, I've been good to me. I've worked hard, invested well. Protected what I've got. At the moment, everything I do and say is aimed at pleasing Cato. That's how I keep what I've got. Of course I'm working to a plan.

DAVID. I never doubted it.

GREGOR. Jealousy's an ugly word. A very negative emotion. But it's not enough that I'm a generous host and a sociable guest. People want to see me take a fall, and they've been waiting for the issue. The more I counsel diplomacy, the more they want to rip Carthage apart. I'm even less popular than I thought. You can tell Cato he better have a plan for phase two, because he's going to have his clamour soon.

DAVID. Money's the problem. It's not hard stirring up people's hatred – there's enough bad history for that. But the cost is putting people off.

GREGOR. Quite the expert.

DAVID. I just listen well.

GREGOR. You must have heard some stuff about me. From your uncle and others.

DAVID. Yes.

GREGOR. I'm not as bad as he thinks.

DAVID. I think he likes you. But people are wrong when they say he rants and raves about all that stuff just to take attention away from other issues. He really believes it. He thinks you're a degenerate. And worse, weak. Luckily for you, he thinks most people are, so he doesn't make it personal.

GREGOR. He disapproves of things I do because he sees it as decadence. A waste of resources. He'd feel the same about any activity that's about fun rather than product. I hate to tell you, but I suspect he considers poetry to be fairly degenerate.

DAVID. He does. I know.

GREGOR. But when I offered to . . . to help you . . . when I offered to help you, do you know what I had in mind? Do you know what I wanted?

DAVID (*uncomfortable*). Not exactly.

GREGOR. I had in mind that we might profitably spend some time together, enjoying each other's company, relaxed and convivial. Like now.

DAVID. This is a business meeting.

GREGOR. Business doesn't have to be work. I keep myself fit and feeling young by enjoying the presence of young people. Some of the things Cato has talked about make me question his own purity. It's a lot more innocent, a lot less harmful than you think.

DAVID. So you never . . .

GREGOR. Never what?

DAVID. You never . . . corrupt them.

GREGOR. What is corruption? To turn something from good to bad, pure to impure . . . where is it written what's good or pure? At a certain age, young men change. Intellectually and physically. To assist and to guide through that change isn't corruption.

DAVID. I meant . . . do you ever . . . physically corrupt them?

GREGOR. Not in the way you've heard about.

DAVID. But you do . . . It's not all like this, talking, being convivial . . . ?

GREGOR. Most of the time it is. But you have nothing to fear from me. You're a man before your time. In my view, you've already been corrupted. Just don't judge me.

DAVID. I can't promise that.

GREGOR (*changing the subject*). You say the cost is putting people off?

DAVID. That's the line you've been taking.

GREGOR. There's a trader I know. He's slightly off the radar, tax-wise, so he owes me a few favours. He says the Carthaginians are rich. Peace has been good to them. That needs to be more widely known. I'll give you his name – pass it on to Marcus. Tell him to make something of it.

DAVID. Why not you?

GREGOR. Marcus is ambitious. I'd like to help him.

DAVID. Really? (*Pause.*) We already know there's money in Carthage. It's just not a reason to go to war. My uncle says it's a security issue, and nothing else.

GREGOR. And he must go on saying it. But we're the Republic of Rome. No one, no one fucks with us. The idea of a poor Carthage being a threat isn't credible. Poor countries don't invade, rich ones do. Get the word out on the wealth and people might believe in the threat to national security. And even if they don't, they'll know at least there's something in it for them. Tell Marcus.

DAVID. I will. And my uncle.

GREGOR. Oh, he knows. He knows.

DAVID. Right. I'll go then.

GREGOR. Yes.

> DAVID *awkwardly re-enacts the embrace from their meeting.*

DAVID. Gregor.

GREGOR. Ah, David!

> *Lights down.*

Scene Three

An area at the side of the stage. MARCUS *is sitting with ledgers.* DAVID *is facing him, looking assured.*

MARCUS. And that's it?

DAVID. That's what he told me.

MARCUS. I ask you to find out what he's up to and you come back with this? A message. No, not just a message. An instruction.

DAVID. It's intelligence.

MARCUS. It's common knowledge. He gave you something he knew we already had. And then tells me to make something of it.

DAVID. I didn't know we had it. If you kept me in the loop more . . .

MARCUS. Use your head. Why would we go to war against a poor country?

DAVID. Trade routes, morale . . .

MARCUS. All right, all right . . . Look, I'm a team player. Gregor's not. I don't ask you to spy on him for my sake. It's important we know what he's up to.

DAVID. My uncle chose him to do a job.

MARCUS. And me. His job is rumour and tittle-tattle; mine is hard strategy. Perhaps you'd better decide what side you're on.

DAVID. The side of Rome, not Carthage. The side of Cato. My uncle.

MARCUS. Oh, I'd forgotten. You're Cato's nephew. Well, in that case, pardon me. Doesn't matter if you do your job or not, then.

DAVID. My job was to be a runner. That's what I'm doing.

MARCUS. Look . . . I'm ambitious. I want to get on. And I've had to fight to get this far. With this face . . . my background . . . I'm here on merit. Gregor's where he is by connections and money. So it comes down to this. What do you want to learn? How to socialise, how to grease palms and spread rumours, how to cover your back, how to live off your family's reputation? Go to the baths, bond on the wrestling mats. Or, if you want to learn real politics, new ways of reading figures, policy management, innovative thinking . . . you stay with me and you work.

DAVID. I . . . Why can't I do both? I like Gregor. He's kind. Funny. But I do want to learn from you. I thought you were . . . just some guy who did what he was told.

MARCUS. I am. And I do it properly. My job is to facilitate conflict in a politically favourable environment. In other words, to plan and co-ordinate strategy. Not to babysit.

DAVID. I might disappoint you, but never say you've had to look after me.

MARCUS. You have to choose. You have Gregor's connections – better – and you have my intellect. Not yet, obviously, but you're bright. What I can't work out is the level of ambition.

DAVID. I heard you in the baths. Before I joined you. You made a fool of yourself.

MARCUS. I know. Cato enjoyed a joke at my expense. So what? I have . . . I have inferiority issues sometimes. I know what I'm like when I'm on a roll. I'm good. Very good. But when I meet important people, and someone like Gregor's so relaxed, contributing so little . . . I get so angry, I overcompensate. It's something I'm working on. (*Pause.*) What would you do if I punched you?

DAVID. Sorry?

MARCUS. If I walked over now and punched you hard in the stomach . . . what would you do?

DAVID. I . . . I don't know.

MARCUS. Well, I'll tell you what you'd do. You'd tell your uncle. Am I right?

DAVID. If . . . if you just punched me . . . for no reason, then yes. You're right. I'd tell my uncle.

MARCUS. What if there was some reason – you'd been lazy, ineffective? Or disrespectful? Not a good reason, but a slight excuse for violence. What then?

DAVID. I'd still tell him.

MARCUS. Of course you would. You understand this is a hypothesis, don't you? You understand I'm not going to actually punch you. Or anything else. I'm not going to throw you around the room, I'm not going to swing a boot into your face, kick you in the balls or break the bridge of your nose with my head. And I'm certainly not going to give that face of yours a couple of cuts with my knife. No. You understand that we are talking . . . hypothetically.

DAVID. Yes. I understand.

MARCUS. Good. Because I'm not a violent person. Not in the slightest. But if I did punch you, hard, in the stomach, and if you did, as you say you would, go running to your uncle, what do you think he would do?

DAVID. You'd wish you were dead.

MARCUS. Perhaps. But I don't think so. You might even get another punch for not fighting back. There's a certain kind of touch, you see, that Cato detests. But it's not the touch of a clenched fist. You've been given a job to do, but I'll be honest – you're not needed. At a certain level, anyone could do it. But it's an opportunity. Cato's giving his nephew an opportunity. To stop with the poetry and become a man. To join his world. So when I tell you to spy on Gregor, I'm inviting you a little further into that world. You're being asked to contribute. Democracy is hard work. We can only go to war after a democratic vote, so you putting everything in danger by not doing your best – well, it's anti-democratic, isn't it?

DAVID. I don't quite see that it is.

MARCUS. Hmm.

He hands over a ledger.

There's to be a meeting tonight. Go to Gregor and give him these – on-the-record statements. Every public utterence made by anyone who matters on the Carthage situation. Or, should I say, the Carthage Crisis. This is the clamour he wanted. On paper. Incontrovertible. We have our opponents, but we know who they are and they're outnumbered. But when the vote happens, we don't want any surprises. We need to know that Gregor is behind us. Take this round there, and try, just try to speak to him.

Lights down.

Scene Four

By the bath. GREGOR *stands, looking at* DAVID.

GREGOR. Well?

DAVID. I brought this. From Marcus.

GREGOR. No. Not that. You've forgotten.

> DAVID, *slightly nervously, walks forward. They embrace.*
> *It's held a little longer.*

DAVID. Gregor.

GREGOR. David. Then break. It's getting late. What's so
important?

DAVID. Documents and stuff. Evidence.

GREGOR. Letting me know what a great job he's doing. I'll
have a look later. (*Casually puts the papers to one side.*)
What else has Marcus been saying to you?

DAVID. Nothing. Not much anyway.

GREGOR. You look . . . you look like you're worried about
something. Normally you seem . . . detached. Something's
eating away at you. I don't know why you should tell me,
but I want to help you. Maybe you've never believed that,
but it's true.

DAVID. Marcus says I have to choose. To be like him or to be
like you.

GREGOR. You couldn't be like me if you tried. Or like him.
That's a compliment. I thought you wanted to be a poet.

DAVID. I do.

GREGOR. Keep that thought. Even if you end up doing
something else, keep hold of that. Any decision you make,
just say to yourself, 'Secretly, I'm a poet.'

DAVID. It's difficult. Remembering I'm a poet when I never
write any poems.

GREGOR. Very few of our poets ever write anything. You'll
be in excellent company. Do you wrestle?

DAVID. Do I what?

GREGOR. Do you wrestle? You know, with your friends. A bit of friendly grip and grapple . . .

DAVID. Sometimes. I used to more often. I don't really enjoy it.

GREGOR. People think it's about force. It's not. It's about balance. Put your hands on my shoulders.

DAVID. Why?

GREGOR. I want to show you something.

DAVID. I don't think we should.

GREGOR. Of course we should. Here.

He takes DAVID*'s arm and places it on his own shoulder. Then the other one.*

Now grip. Your aim is to stop me coming towards you.

DAVID *does so.*

You see? You lean forward. Automatically. If you're upright, or leaning back, it's easier for me to push you over. But if you come towards me a little, it's easier for you to stand your ground. Now let's say I want to lift you by the leg.

He moves forward and makes a grab for DAVID*'s leg.* DAVID *moves back,* GREGOR *stumbles forward, clutching air. He stands up.*

You see? You give a little, you keep your balance and wait for others to lose theirs. Go with your uncle for now, but stay in control. Make sure you're the one on your feet. Does that make sense?

DAVID. I think so. Yes.

GREGOR. Good. Again.

They grip, and circle for a while, shifting weight. This time, when he makes his move, GREGOR *is quicker. He feigns to go for the leg again, then breaks, and as* DAVID *moves backwards quickly spins and bear-hugs him, lifts him off the ground, makes to slam him onto the floor – but instead*

gently lowers him, till they are both sitting on the floor,
DAVID *still gripped by* GREGOR.

DAVID. You're stronger than me. That isn't balance, that's you
being stronger than me.

GREGOR. I know. I'm not hurting you, am I?

DAVID. No. I'm OK.

GREGOR. It's just a warning. When you pull away from
people like Marcus or your uncle, try not to let them know
it was you who made them stumble. Because if they come
back with force . . . Well, poets rarely win.

DAVID. I should go.

GREGOR. Stay a while.

DAVID. No. You're right . . . I'm not supposed to . . . to be
with you like this.

GREGOR. We had a wrestle. There's nothing wrong with that.
And we're not going to do anything else. But . . . Well, you
make me feel I could have been a poet, instead of . . . this.

DAVID. No. I should go.

GREGOR. Stay. I'm not seducing you. I mean everything I say.

DAVID. We'll both be in trouble.

GREGOR. You don't believe me. Look, I'm not seducing you
because it's not something I do. I don't do seduction. If
I want a fuck, I pay for it. That's not what I want here. It's
a completely . . . a completely different thing. Not a thing
I can put into words. Maybe you can, if you feel any of it.
But I'm happier here, holding you, than I have been for
years. I want to hold you for ever. Do you understand?

DAVID. Yes.

GREGOR *kisses the top of* DAVID's *head.* CATO *enters.*
He watches for a while. DAVID *notices first. He breaks*
from GREGOR *and gets up quickly.*

Uncle . . .

GREGOR. Cato . . .

CATO *says nothing*. GREGOR *gets up, slowly*.

We were . . . wrestling.

DAVID. It was my idea. I wanted . . . to learn.

CATO. Go, David.

DAVID. We were just . . .

CATO. Go now. Go to your father. I'll be round presently. But for now, just go. Go without saying a word. A single word. Understand?

DAVID *exits*. GREGOR *and* CATO *look at each other*. GREGOR *breaks first*.

GREGOR. That wasn't what it seemed. (*Pause*.) It probably looked different from what it was. (*Laughs*.) It must have looked quite funny – I can see how you misread the situation.

CATO. Shut up.

GREGOR. No, really, I understand.

CATO. Shut up. You understand nothing. You don't understand what the expression 'off limits' means. You don't understand that if a man like me threatens to cut off your balls, that is what will happen.

GREGOR. Nothing happened.

CATO. Perhaps that's true. Perhaps David was lucky. But I see the intent in your eyes.

GREGOR. I'm fond of him. So what? Relax.

CATO. Don't tell me to fucking relax. I don't know if I should kill you myself or let the law take its course. Messing about with a free-born youth . . .

GREGOR. We wrestled. There's no crime.

CATO. It would ruin you.

GREGOR. If you want it badly enough, yes. I suppose it might. There'd be quite a fuss. Consul's nephew and senator . . . The gossip . . . You wouldn't be immune – introducing us. Certainly, it'll take people's minds off Carthage. Is that what you want? So close to getting your war and you're going to blow it all for a chance to have a shot at me? Focus, Cato, that's what you're lacking.

Pause. CATO *smiles.*

CATO. Maybe I did get it wrong. Yes . . . it would be foolish to waste a resource like you, Gregor. Foolish.

GREGOR. Thank you.

CATO. Of course, you'll never see him again. I imagine he'll get a bit of a thrashing, then my brother will send him away for a while. Toughen him up.

GREGOR. There's no need. For any of that. You think that if you hurt him, you'll hurt me. Maybe you would. But there's no need. I had no wish to anger you. I'll not speak to him again.

CATO. I know you won't speak to him again. You won't be able to. Because you won't be here. You'll be in Carthage.

GREGOR. Carthage . . . I'm not a soldier.

CATO. No, you're not, are you? You're many things, Gregor, but you're not a soldier. Sometimes I look around the Senate and I think about the years of contribution, the acts of bravery in the field, everything that's been achieved by the men in that building. And then I see you. How did you get there?

GREGOR. I got there because people wanted me there. You might not like it, but the people seem to think it worthwhile to have a few people representing them who aren't campaigning on their war record.

CATO. You're no man of peace, Gregor. Every vote you cast, every rumour you start . . . these acts kill as many men as a soldier's sword.

GREGOR. I know it. I've done everything you've asked and you've almost got your war. So leave me here and finish the thing off. I'm no use to you in Carthage.

CATO. We'll see. I'm going to give you a very special commission. It's an honour; you can't possibly turn it down.

GREGOR. Cato . . .

CATO. Please understand something. I'm not sending you to
　　Carthage as a piece of military strategy. I'm sending you
　　because I don't want to see your face for a year. I'm sending
　　you because I want to hurt you. You crossed me – no,
　　worse, you directly disobeyed me, and you're going to
　　pay. Probably the other generals will moan at me. 'Anybody
　　but him', I imagine, will be the common response. But you
　　might have your uses. Not during the fighting, obviously,
　　but after . . . it's then that things can get messy. Follow the
　　leads, track down the wealth . . . follow instructions and
　　you might get back in my good books. Show some strength
　　of mind, some spirit. And see what you started. Experience
　　it yourself.

GREGOR. My strength is in Rome. My contacts. I can be
　　useful to you.

CATO. The fight here is won. I need you over there.

GREGOR. Please.

CATO. No. I've made my decision. You've encouraged a
　　clamour, you've helped consign Carthage to history. And
　　why?

GREGOR. To please you.

CATO. No. So you can carry on. Carthage must be destroyed,
　　not for the good of Rome, but so that you can carry on with
　　your wine, with your baths and your boys. You'll find them
　　a coarse bunch in the army. Less refined than you're used
　　to. You're going to live with what you helped create. I look
　　forward to regular dispatches from you. Perhaps being an
　　outsider might have its advantages. You'll be less inclined
　　to overlook any failure of duty. And if you come back, job
　　done, then maybe you'll think twice before spitting in the
　　face of the people that allow you your luxuries.

GREGOR. If I come back?

CATO. I don't know why, but I rather hope you do. That you
　　prove me wrong. Because wars are difficult, Gregor. All
　　wars are difficult. You'll see things that will make you
　　retch, and your fellow generals will laugh at you for your
　　weakness. Maybe you'll step up, make a contribution. Earn
　　your lifestyle. We'll see.

MARCUS *enters*.

MARCUS. Am I interrupting something?

CATO. Not at all. I have just been giving Gregor here an important commission.

MARCUS. A commission? What commission?

CATO. Gregor's going to be my man in Carthage. Provide regular reports on the other generals and take care of the post-war strategy. It's an important job, and it's no more than you deserve.

MARCUS. I thought I . . .

CATO. You thought what?

MARCUS. Nothing. I won't hide it – I was hoping for something like that myself. But congratulations, Gregor. I know you'll do the job well.

GREGOR. Thank you. (*Recovering himself*.) And thank you, Cato. It's an honour. I won't let Rome down.

CATO. Just what I wanted to hear. Don't worry, Marcus. I have plans for you. You've shown talent and industry – I can use that. But for this job I need somebody with . . . Gregor's status and reputation.

MARCUS. I understand. Perfectly.

CATO. Now Rome is waiting for action. Tomorrow I shall give them what they want. I would like you to hear my speech.

MARCUS. With respect, sir . . . with all respect, I have heard your speech. It doesn't work.

CATO. You've heard my speech? Explain.

MARCUS. You have a tendency, I've noticed, to rehearse your speeches under the guise of off-the-cuff remarks – testing a phrase or a quotation on a few of us to see if we respond well. Unfortunately, most people around you would applaud you sneezing. What you've prepared for tomorrow night is too measured, too sophisticated. You need to be more direct. It's not enough for us to go to war. You have to be remembered as the one who took us there.

Pause.

CATO. When did you acquire teeth?

MARCUS. I've always had them. But a while ago a man gave me some advice. He told me not to put all my eggs in Cato's basket. Well, I ignored that advice. I need this to work now, and if arguing a little – asserting myself more – is the way for me to make sure that happens, then I will do so.

CATO. I should hope so. Well . . . if you can be civil about it, I have no problem with frankness. But it's too late to do anything about the speech.

MARCUS (*produces speech*). Actually, I have taken the liberty of . . . of giving you another option.

CATO. You've written me a speech.

MARCUS. Yes.

CATO. That's so impertinent. (*Laughs.*) Let's have a look at it, then. (*Takes* MARCUS*'s speech.*) Welcome to the inner circle.

Lights down.

Scene Five

CATO *delivers his speech downstage centre.* MARCUS *is to the right, watching, appraising.*

CATO. Fellow Romans.

You have heard me speak to you before about the evil that dwells within our midst; the evil of moral turpitude. Some of you did not like my message. Some of you chose instead to insist on a right to behave without regard to the greater good of society; to slake your thirst at the well of licentiousness; to dine out on the table of debauchery. Some of you thought that because Rome was strong, you may be weak.

But, Romans, the strength of the Republic is the strength of its citizens. And when the weakness of the few becomes the weakness of the many, the Republic itself is weakened.

Now, it seems, others have noticed. Carthage – yes, that same Carthage that our grandfathers defeated – Carthage now looks at Rome and sees weakness. And so Carthage wants what we have. Those of you who know me know that I am slow to anger. I do not rush in on gossip and hearsay. An overseas expedition requires courage, forbearance and investment, and I would not ask these of you lightly. But it is needed. On your behalf I have used my best men and I have hard evidence, Romans, of Carthaginian stockpiling of munitions. Their wealth has been under-represented, and their offensive intent is clear. They are a threat, and threats must be destroyed.

Carthage must be destroyed.

Carthage must be destroyed, so Rome will prosper.

Carthage must be destroyed or Rome will wither and die.

Am I serious? Is the matter as grave as this? People, we are the Republic of Rome. If our enemies think to raid us of our ports, then our enemies' friends will soon be knocking on the door. If a chariot loses a wheel, its driver will fail to finish the race. If a trader loses his merchandise, his family will go hungry. And if a republic loses its land, its people will be slaves. The Carthaginians may limit themselves in the beginning to land-grabs and naval strikes, but they want more. They want it all. They want your house, your land, your family. But I won't give them what they want. I am slow to anger, but I am angry. Carthage has threatened my people. Carthage must be destroyed.

Fifty years ago, Asdrubal and Hannibal caused pain and misery to our Republic. The war came right to the heart of our lands. The Rome that we know and love was as close to its own destruction as ever before or since. We defeated them, but we were generous in our victory. I vow to you, Romans, that this will not happen again. Why should we wait to be invaded? We know their plans. There is an obvious present danger to our security, so we will go to them. And we will not be generous. They have had their chance. And we have learnt our lesson. Carthage must not be taken lightly – Carthage must not be given second chances. Carthage must be destroyed.

Carthage

Must

Be

Destroyed.

Lights out.

End of Act One.

ACT TWO

Carthage, 146 BC

Scene One

The roof of a residential building on the outskirts of Carthage.
An awning for shade. Fairly comfortable, with two benches for
seating. Some rope in the corner. It is the middle of the afternoon,
and hot. GREGOR *looks rough. He is standing, looking out*
towards Carthage, near the edge of the roof. A YOUTH *is*
lying on a bench, apparently asleep.

GREGOR. Wake up. (*Louder.*) I said wake up.

YOUTH. I am awake.

GREGOR. Come here.

YOUTH (*after a pause*). No.

GREGOR. I have to show you something.

YOUTH. I'm tired.

GREGOR. If you come here, I can be gentle. If you stay where
you are, it's difficult.

YOUTH. I don't understand what you're talking about.

GREGOR. I can see smoke. I think your city is on fire. Yes.
Carthage is . . . is on fire.

YOUTH *gets up and joins* GREGOR.

I'm sorry.

YOUTH. There's some smoke. A building or two. But not a
city. You're exaggerating.

GREGOR. I think this is it. I think this is the day.

YOUTH. We've seen fires before.

GREGOR. Yes, but . . . it feels different today.

YOUTH. To me it feels the same. The same as every other day
in the who-knows-how-many months. Wake up, eat, come
up here, sleep, eat. The only difference is a bit of smoke.

GREGOR. I understand. You're worried about your family.

YOUTH *returns to his bench.*

That's only natural. I should go. Find out what's happening.

YOUTH. But you won't.

GREGOR. Of course I will.

YOUTH. You won't go because you never do go. Every three
months you talk about it. Once you even put your boots on.
But you never leave.

GREGOR. You say that critically. But my inaction had a lot
of thought behind it. If this is the start, I should be there.
I have a duty.

YOUTH. You do. You should go.

GREGOR. I know.

YOUTH. You must leave the door unlocked.

GREGOR. You'd escape.

YOUTH. Yes, but if you go and . . . It might be dangerous. If
something happened to you, I'd starve to death.

GREGOR. Nothing would happen to me.

YOUTH. I'd decompose.

GREGOR. I'll be quite safe.

YOUTH. Pecked at by birds.

GREGOR. We'll see. There's no need for me to go right this
minute. I'll monitor the situation. Make a decision later.

He goes to a bench and pours himself a beaker of wine.

YOUTH. You won't go anywhere.

GREGOR. I know that's what you think. You've been quite
clear. So I'm not even going to convince you you're wrong.
I'll just enjoy the look on your face when I stroll out the
door. Leaving you here.

YOUTH. We'll see, you said.

GREGOR. I did, yes. But you're being . . . well, you're being rude today, to be frank. You're often a little difficult, but I make allowances. I know the situation is difficult.

YOUTH. Being a prisoner.

GREGOR. Being a hostage, yes. Exactly. It can't be easy, so I'm tolerant those times when, well, when you let yourself down a little.

YOUTH. When I what?

GREGOR. When you let yourself down. A little.

YOUTH. I'm given as a hostage, taken from the others and imprisoned here for two years, and you think sometimes my manners let me down?

GREGOR. A little, yes. I see the point you're making, and I sympathise. But your family are Carthaginian nobility. You owe it to them, surely, to conduct yourself properly at all times.

YOUTH. I only said that you wouldn't leave here. My family wouldn't want me to lie. You'll finish that jug, working out your plan to leave, then you'll start another one, and then you'll fall asleep.

GREGOR. It's hardly your place to pass comment on my drinking. But if it seems that I'm a little overfond of the stuff, then bear in mind that that has been in the context of me not having much to do. If that situation changes, you'll see a very different Gregor.

YOUTH. A man of action?

GREGOR. Indeed. That smoke might just be the start of something. A new phase. I hope so.

YOUTH. It has been a long time since you . . . did anything.

GREGOR. I don't deny it. And it may be that I decide that the best policy is to sit it out a little longer. Let the final days play out their course. My strengths aren't really in the combat zone.

YOUTH. So now you're not going.

GREGOR. I'm saying nothing's been decided. (*Drinks*.)

YOUTH. Can I have a drink?

GREGOR. It's been a long time since you asked me that.

YOUTH. I know.

GREGOR. Months. But I've explained why it's out of the question.

YOUTH. You have, yes.

GREGOR. You know it's nothing to do with meanness or protocol. In many ways I'd like to have a drink with you.

YOUTH. I know. It's because you like my face.

GREGOR. That makes it sound like the rule is for my benefit. It's not about me, it's about you. You have a lovely complexion. That's a fact. The problem with wine in this type of situation is that it's very easy to start drinking a bit too much almost every day. Which is a nightmare for the skin. I don't want to be responsible for you being . . . blotchy.

YOUTH. Thank you. It's just that . . . if you're right, if that smoke is significant, then this will be over soon. I won't be able to ruin my skin. There won't be time.

Pause.

GREGOR. Do you drink at home? Are you allowed?

YOUTH. I'm not at home.

GREGOR. That's my point. I consider myself, I don't know how to put it, a . . . a replacement parent. Not a father, I know you'd hate that. But if you'd let me, I could be the uncle you're parcelled off to for the summer. It's not a normal situation, I agree, but in a way your parents did put you in my trust. I'm not about to abuse that trust. In fact, I take it very seriously.

YOUTH. You believe that?

GREGOR. There's been no mistreatment. No violence.

YOUTH. You demanded three hundred hostages before you would even negotiate. All my people wanted to do was

surrender. If . . . if you're not abusing that trust, I don't
know what I'm still doing here.

GREGOR. Look, politics is a messy business. It's not got a lot
to do with trust. In fact, if you could do one thing for me,
it would be this. Every time you talk about this . . . this
situation, and you say 'you' – 'You did this', 'You did that'
– change it to 'your people': 'Your people did this'.
Between the two of us, I'm not altogether happy about taking
personal responsibility for everything my people have done
here.

YOUTH. What things?

GREGOR. I don't know. (*Pause*.) That's the point. I don't
really know what's going on.

YOUTH. You're a general and a senator in the Republic of
Rome.

GREGOR. I know.

YOUTH. Yet you never leave here.

GREGOR. I know.

YOUTH. You need a secretary, but you write no letters.

GREGOR. I look after you. Don't I?

YOUTH. For now, yes.

GREGOR. If your father walked in right now, I could shake
his hand, embrace him as a friend and hand you over.

YOUTH. He would probably kill you before you could speak.

Pause.

GREGOR. Maybe. And maybe that's right. If I were him . . .
perhaps that's what I'd do. Because how could he know?
How could he know that I'm protecting you? What sense
could that make? And yet I want to. Even little things, like
you wanting a drink. I could just say, 'Yes, go on, help
yourself. There's tons of it.' Or I could say, 'No way. It's
mine. Remember where you are.' But I don't do either. I try
and be reasonable. What would your father want me to do?

YOUTH. He'd want you to let me go.

GREGOR. I'm trying to be patient; it's clear I'm talking about drinking. I can be a steadying parental hand in some ways. But not in others.

YOUTH. My parents let me drink.

GREGOR. Good. Excellent. We can have a drink together.

He pours two beakers.

Here. Your health.

YOUTH. To Carthage.

GREGOR. Yes, of course. To Carthage. With, in my case, qualifications. And to Rome, with the same. I assume it's a social drink they let you have. You're not allowed to get drunk, are you?

YOUTH. No, not really.

GREGOR. In some ways a shame. I could imagine a real session with you. Getting slowly rat-arsed, putting the world to rights. If international politics was run by well-meaning drunken fools there wouldn't be any wars, no killing or destruction. Just little flare-ups followed by hugs and tears. But you've not had a drink for a long time. You'd get drunk too quickly. The really good sessions are when two men of like mind get together who are evenly paced. It doesn't matter if they get rat-arsed in an hour or six hours. But they have to be evenly paced. I fancy I have a different pace from you.

YOUTH. You have had a head start.

GREGOR. That's true. I have. There's a condition.

YOUTH. What?

GREGOR. Well, you convinced me. That the situation was now different. So I showed flexibility. Our relationship has changed.

YOUTH. Unless I'm free to leave, nothing has changed.

GREGOR. But it has. You're right about the basic dynamic, I grant you. But it's still a very significant shift when two people suddenly find they're drinking together. It means . . .

it means I can feel, once again, free to ask you to do something for me.

YOUTH. No.

GREGOR. You don't know what it is yet.

YOUTH. Yes I do. And no.

GREGOR. We're drinking together.

YOUTH. It doesn't matter.

GREGOR. Please. Tell me your name.

Silence.

Tell me.

Silence.

You have your reasons, I suppose. They're important to you. But look: neither of us knows what's going to happen. There are a lot of possibilities. But I intend to look out for you. Somewhere, soon, you'll be a man. And a man needs to be able to have a chat. To converse. It's important. I've made it a priority all my life to learn people's names. And to remember them. To ask about their family, their problems, their enthusiasms. To get to know them.

YOUTH. Do you have a family?

GREGOR. Excellent. A question. You're learning. Do I have a family? Yes. Yes, I do.

YOUTH. Is that it?

GREGOR. I like them.

YOUTH. Just 'like'?

GREGOR. They bring a sense of responsibility to me. Without them I could easily just chuck the whole game in. I don't need a villa, I don't need to entertain. I'm a man of simple pleasures.

YOUTH. Do you love them?

GREGOR. Yes. In my own way.

YOUTH. Do you miss them?

GREGOR. Very much. (*Drinks*.) And I miss my garden. I miss strolling in my garden.

YOUTH. At least, when you return, your family and garden will still be there. That's why this cannot be a proper conversation. Because we are not the same, and soon you will be strolling in your garden. If you want to call me by my name, then give me a name. Is that not the way with slaves?

GREGOR. You are not a slave. You are a noble hostage. You keep your name. I want you to keep your name.

YOUTH. I 'work' as your secretary. I'm not free to leave. For a year I slept in chains. How am I not a slave?

GREGOR. For a year, yes. But then a trust developed.

YOUTH. I'm locked in. Trust?

GREGOR. I can't help the locked door. That's you. You promised not to attack me, I throw away the chains. But you wouldn't promise not to escape. I was prepared to accept your word. Look, war throws up situations. You're part of a situation you have no control over. So am I.

YOUTH. When we were all waiting in the main hall, waiting to go wherever the others went – a prison perhaps, or a fort, or a mass grave – and you called me . . . you were different then, confident. You had authority. Do you remember how you addressed me?

GREGOR. No. I hope I was civil.

YOUTH. You clapped your hands and said, 'Hey, youth. Come here.'

GREGOR. That sounds reasonable enough. It sounds like me.

YOUTH. I felt like a dog.

GREGOR. I was a bit . . . abrupt, maybe. In retrospect. But I didn't know your name. I still don't. I don't want to call you 'Youth' any more.

YOUTH. But you must. To remind you that the . . . the situation hasn't changed. I am still not free to go. I am still apart from my family. Say what you want, I'm still a slave.

GREGOR (*calmly takes* YOUTH*'s wine back*). I'm more likely
to give a beating to a slave than a beaker of my own wine.
Every time I think we're getting somewhere close to . . . to
a reasonable working relationship, you start moaning. Yes,
you've been unlucky. That's established. But I let you say
things to me that others would thrash you close to death for.

YOUTH. I've always known that, if that was your will, that
was what I would get.

GREGOR. But it wasn't my will. We were talking and
drinking wine. You're the one who spoilt all that.

YOUTH. Why did you choose me?

GREGOR. You've lost the right to ask me questions.

YOUTH. I never had the right. It suited you to talk about
yourself. I want to know why you chose me.

GREGOR. Would you rather be with the others?

YOUTH. Why wouldn't I be? People I know, people my own
age, held on a promise of honour. I know my people were
going to surrender. We had no choice. That would mean the
hostages were safe. So why wouldn't I rather be with them?
Or do you know something I don't?

GREGOR. That's another example of the sort of tone – not the
remark as such, but the tone – that would really lead others
to lose their patience.

YOUTH. But how can you know anything? No one comes in
here except to give you food. Oh and wine. Always more
wine. You don't *do* anything.

GREGOR. That's enough.

YOUTH. You're finished. They don't trust you.

GREGOR *punches* YOUTH *in the stomach.* YOUTH
collapses forward, into GREGOR*'s arms.* GREGOR *holds
him.*

GREGOR. Look what you made me do. Look what you made
me do. I'm sorry. You've been asking for that, but I never
thought you'd get it. A reason to hate me.

He lays YOUTH *on a rug.*

Just rest. Take some time. Maybe now, I have to let you go. If that's what you want, and I know it will be.

He holds YOUTH *for a while, then heads for the table to collect* YOUTH*'s wine. As he is about to pick it up,* MARCUS *enters.*

MARCUS. It's a bit early for wine, isn't it?

GREGOR. Marcus . . .

MARCUS. I'd have thought being a general representing the Republic of Rome in an overseas expedition necessitated a clear head. The ability to make quick decisions, unimpaired by alcohol.

GREGOR. It's weak stuff, really.

MARCUS. Still . . . clouds the judgement, my friend. How are you?

They embrace, formally.

GREGOR. I'm . . . I'm OK.

MARCUS (*sitting down in front of* YOUTH, *not noticing him*). It's all got a bit messy, hasn't it . . .

GREGOR. What do you mean?

MARCUS. Well, you're still here. You must be missing Rome. Must've thought you'd be back by now.

GREGOR. I was wondering . . .

MARCUS. I certainly didn't expect to find myself here. But . . . one has to try and turn things into one's advantage. There's been a few cock-ups, that's for sure, and – to be blunt – if I can sort it out, it should help me get up the ladder.

GREGOR. Looks like you're already doing quite well for yourself.

MARCUS. I'll say one thing for Cato. He recognises achievement. Thing is, Gregor, some people are going to come out of this well and some aren't. I want to make sure you're all right. I don't owe you anything, but . . . well, we started this, in a way. You've not exactly done your job, but

I still think you'd make a bad enemy. So if I can keep you
out of things, I will. But first, I need to look after myself.
There's no way I'm taking the fall for this.

GREGOR. How could anyone blame you?

MARCUS. Financially, this is my war. I costed it. When the
serious opposition was about money, I was the one who got
the books to balance. A few exaggerations on the likely
spoils of war, that sort of thing. But for the plan to really
work, we needed to be sure of one thing.

GREGOR (*defiantly taking a drink, trying to regain control*).
Enlighten me.

MARCUS. There wasn't supposed to be a war, Gregor. There
wasn't supposed to be any fighting at all. Carthage wasn't
a threat; there wouldn't be any opposition. We'd be in and
out, leaving the place razed to the fucking ground. Our
pockets, and the Republic's coffers, just a bit better off and
a nice away win for the supporters. How come we're
fighting, Gregor? How come we're losing men?

GREGOR. I don't . . . I don't like your tone.

MARCUS. And I don't like being made to look a fool. This
is costing us money and lives, and it wasn't supposed to.
So, Gregor, our man in Carthage, excuse me for being a bit
pissed off, but perhaps, as you sip your wine, you could
explain to me what your take on all this is.

GREGOR. My take?

MARCUS. Yes. Your version of events. From the outside, it's
easy to criticise. You've been here. Your reports have not
reached Rome – that can happen. So now . . . here I am.
Tell me what's going on.

GREGOR (*still trying to work out what's happened*). We
followed the plan. After the army landed, a plea to surrender
came in straight away. It was almost embarrassing.

MARCUS. We knew that would happen. What then?

GREGOR. We demanded three hundred young nobles as
hostages, to be kept at Utica, while negotiations for the
surrender took place.

MARCUS. Arrangements. You don't negotiate with these
people, you make arrangements. But so far, according to the
plan. What next?

GREGOR. We demanded all their weapons before they could
hear our demands. Which I thought was laying it on a bit
thick, but what do I know? They moaned a bit, said it was
unfair. But they did.

MARCUS. So. Everyone follows Cato's plan – you have three
hundred hostages and all their weapons.

GREGOR. Yes. Couldn't have gone smoother really. Then we
told them, 'Get your stuff and leave the city. It is the will of
Rome that it be burnt to the ground.' Serious unhappiness
all around, but back they went to tell their people.

MARCUS. Job done. You must have been very happy.

GREGOR. Yes. I suppose so. Well . . . yes; pleased to have
served Cato and the Republic. Not much of a victory,
though. Not really. It's hard to be happy, exactly, about
burning a city to the ground.

MARCUS. You saw it burn?

GREGOR. No. I came here. To wait.

MARCUS. To wait.

GREGOR. Yes. There didn't seem much point in being around
until after the deed had been done.

MARCUS (*walks over to the edge to look out towards
Carthage*). And from here you'd be able to see. To watch
Carthage burn and know when to come back and do your
job.

GREGOR. Yes.

MARCUS. You chose well. An excellent vantage point. You
can see the smoke quite clearly. And flames, just a few.
(*Turns back towards* GREGOR.) I'm tired. I've had a long
journey.

GREGOR. Of course. You want to rest. Understandable. We
can talk later.

MARCUS. No. I don't want to rest. I'm just pointing it out. I've had a long journey. I've come from Rome.

GREGOR. I know.

MARCUS. Things started going pear-shaped over here, messages reach Cato in Rome – I repeat, in Rome – I travel from Rome, to here, to sort it out. You're five miles away, you know the city's not been destroyed but you won't travel five miles to find out what's happening. What the fuck's been going on?

GREGOR. You . . . you can't speak to me like that.

MARCUS. Get a grip on things, Gregor. It's not like that any more. I can speak to you how I like. Without me, you're finished. Perhaps even with me.

GREGOR. All right. I'll tell you the truth. I . . . I've not been well. Not for a long time. That's why I didn't want to come here in the first place. It was nothing to do with . . . Of course I wanted to serve, however I could. I tried. I was at Utica. Everything seemed to be going fine. I felt . . . I didn't feel myself. So I came here. Close enough to Carthage if I was needed but just a bit quieter. People knew where I was. They should have come to me if there was a problem.

MARCUS. They did come for you, Gregor. I can't help you if you're going to lie. How do you think I found this place? I asked around. I asked the others. Most of them had been here, to get you. But you wouldn't see anyone.

GREGOR. I . . . I might have turned someone away. Once. I seem to remember . . . Like I say, I haven't been well.

MARCUS. You've done nothing but drink. There's a Roman cook here just for you. It's a disgrace.

GREGOR. My only staff. He comes once a day, that's all.

MARCUS. I'm sorry. I don't see what I can do for you. I thought . . . I thought there must be a reason. It's you, Gregor. I mean, I've never liked you. I've never liked the way you do business, the way you put yourself before the state, but this . . . You were always an operator. Now you're just lost.

GREGOR. I can get it back. I was a bit lost for a while, that's all. Don't tell Cato. I'll get my act together . . . And I'll owe you. You'll have a good war, I'll have a bad one, but I could still be useful to you.

MARCUS. I doubt that. But it's not an option.

GREGOR. You don't want it to be an option. You're the one with Cato's ear. You could do this for me.

MARCUS. Normally, yes. But Cato's here.

GREGOR. Here?

MARCUS. I can't believe how little you know. This is big. His job's on the line. Of course he's here. He's with the generals in Carthage, but I know he wants to see you.

GREGOR. Right. Get me up to speed. I can rescue this. (*Drinks.*) I know I can. Smarten up, tell a tale . . . I've been here before.

MARCUS. He'll speak to the same people I spoke to. There's only one thing working in your favour. Cato didn't exactly expect you to lead the Roman army. He thought you had your uses in Rome, but not here.

GREGOR. I know. I know that. I've felt . . . unmotivated. So I might not be the scapegoat?

MARCUS. Not the only one. But he's still angry. You were to be . . .

GREGOR. His eyes and ears.

MARCUS. That's all he wanted.

GREGOR. I've let him down.

MARCUS. That's the way he sees it. Your job was to tell him what was happening. And what was not happening.

GREGOR. Not happening . . .

MARCUS. The army gave the Carthaginians time to leave their homes. A humane, civilised decision. But how much bloody time did they need? Our soldiers kicked their heels for a couple of days before marching. I say marching. It was more of a saunter. They fucking ambled into town.

From what we can make out, the people of Carthage had more guts than their leaders. Really angry with them for giving up their weapons. They'd been up day and night making arms. The women were cutting off their hair to make strings for the bows. By the time the army got there, every fortress was armed. So instead of a quick in-and-out, we had a siege. An expensive, messy and unneccessary siege.

GREGOR. Why wasn't I told?

MARCUS. Maybe you were drunk and forgot. Maybe you didn't tell anyone to tell you. Maybe people thought, 'He's a Roman general. At some point he'll leave his fucking room.'

YOUTH (*standing up*). I knew it.

MARCUS. Who the fuck is that?

YOUTH. I always knew.

MARCUS. Gregor. Would you please tell me what the fuck is going on?

YOUTH. They would never surrender.

MARCUS. You. Shut up. Get back down on the floor. Over there. (*Points downstage.*) Now – (*To* GREGOR.) Tell me what's happening here.

GREGOR. He's . . . he's a hostage.

MARCUS. He's a hostage. For crying out loud . . . I see what's going on. You're sent abroad. You go into a sulk, sort yourself out for food and booze . . . and a boy. Cato's going to hang you out to dry.

GREGOR. He needn't know.

MARCUS. He will cut your balls off this time.

GREGOR. Only if you tell him.

YOUTH. Death to the Roman invader.

MARCUS. Right, you little shit.

He walks over to YOUTH *and kicks him hard in the face.*

GREGOR. No, Marcus. You bastard.

He lunges at MARCUS *and tries to wrestle him to the
ground.* MARCUS *is too quick, too good, uses* GREGOR*'s
momentum to march him to the edge of the roof.*

MARCUS. It's a fair way down. Might be survivable. Fancy
your chances?

GREGOR. No.

MARCUS. Then calm down. Sit.

He points to a bench. GREGOR *sits.* MARCUS *studies*
YOUTH, *who has blood running down his face.*

Not so pretty now, is he? You're out of shape, old man. You
should do more exercise, get out more. Anyone would think
you'd been sitting on your arse for a year or two. Lay a
finger on me again and I'll kill him in front of you.

GREGOR. He was worried about his family. That's all. He
didn't think what he was saying. There was no need . . . Let
me check he's OK. (*Starts to get up.*)

MARCUS. Just stay where you are. I've had it with you.
Going after Cato's nephew . . . that's the stupidest thing I've
seen for a while. Fooling around with a Carthaginian . . .
It's sick. We're at war with them.

GREGOR. I didn't know that.

MARCUS. His people are killing our soldiers. While you're . . .

GREGOR. He's my secretary. I needed a secretary.

MARCUS. What for? Show me the work.

GREGOR. OK . . . I thought I needed a secretary. Perhaps
I don't. But he does no harm. I thought he might provide
information.

MARCUS. He might provide information? Excellent. I know
just the people to get to work on that smooth skin of his.
He'll tell us this information in half an hour. Though we
might spin it out if we're enjoying it.

GREGOR. No . . .

MARCUS. Things are different. Sometimes you have to charge
it up a little.

GREGOR. He's just a boy. A young man. I don't even know his name.

MARCUS (*picking up a beaker*). Yet he too can drink wine while all around him his people are sacrificing their lives. You two deserve each other.

GREGOR. No. He's better than me. He wanted to leave. I wanted to stay.

MARCUS. He wanted to leave, did he? We can't have that.

MARCUS *goes over to* YOUTH, *takes his dagger out and quickly, deftly, cuts across one of* YOUTH's *hamstrings.* YOUTH *yells with pain as blood spurts out.* MARCUS *wipes his dagger on* YOUTH's *clothes.*

GREGOR. No!

MARCUS. He's a hostage. His people haven't exactly played ball. Now he's a slave. I don't want him going anywhere.

GREGOR. Animal!

MARCUS. I'm getting out of this mess, and I'll do what I have to do. Cato will turn up. He's negotiating with the fortresses. As soon as they open the gates to let the women and children out, that's it, over.

GREGOR. You're all animals.

MARCUS. They had a choice. I'm going to make sure everything's on schedule. Carthage must be destroyed. If you've any sense you'll come with me . . . be seen with a few people. He's not going anywhere.

GREGOR. Just go.

MARCUS (*picks up a beaker and drains it*). It's not even good stuff. Look after each other.

MARCUS *exits.*

YOUTH *is whimpering.*

GREGOR. If only you'd told me your name, Youth. I could comfort you.

He kneels in front of YOUTH, *cradling his bloodied head.*

Your people were brave, Youth, just as you said. Think about them. (*Pause*.) You asked me why I chose you. I can't say. I hadn't meant to choose anyone. But you caught my eye. Your skin reminded me of someone. Of a hundred young men, but one in particular. Your face . . . your complexion. I'm sorry, Youth. I'm sorry you caught my eye. Your nose is broken. Your jaw is bruised. They will get better. You'll be . . . beautiful . . . again. And your leg . . . we'll get a doctor. It might not be so bad.

GREGOR *props* YOUTH *up, covers him with a blanket, goes and pours himself some wine. He stops, and tries to get* YOUTH *to drink it instead. No luck.*

I'll leave it there. Drink it, when you can.

He pours himself one. Drinks pensively, as if making a decision.

There's no safe place I can take you. I'm going into Carthage. It's night soon. I'm making you a promise, Youth. I'm going to find your parents. Rescue them. I don't know if you can hear me, but I know if you can you'll . . . you'll think I probably don't mean it, and even if I do I won't be able to. But I used to be someone. I can do this. (*Pause*.) If you tell me your name . . . (*Pause*.) You're nobility. Give me a name and I will find your family. They will come for you. I want to do this. For you.

YOUTH *whimpers something undecipherable.*

What? What was that?

With supreme effort, YOUTH *sits up and focuses on* GREGOR.

YOUTH. Hanb . . .

GREGOR. Hanb?

YOUTH (*clearly*). Hannibal.

GREGOR. I will find them.

Lights down.

Scene Two

A few hours later. The sun is beginning to set. CATO *enters. Looks around.*

CATO. Gregor . . . Gregor . . . (*Notices* YOUTH.) Who the hell are you?

YOUTH (*speaking with difficulty*). No name.

CATO. No name, eh . . . (*Notices wine.*) Are you drunk?

YOUTH. No.

CATO. Good. I can't abide drunkenness. Deserter?

YOUTH. No.

CATO. Thank goodness for that. Lowest of the low, deserters. I'm tracking one down. So, you're just a young Carthaginian caught up in the madness. Someone's landed you a blow.

YOUTH. It hurts.

CATO. Doesn't look much more than a punch in the face. Good one, mind, but a lad your age should be able to take it.

YOUTH. My leg.

CATO. Your leg.

YOUTH. Yes.

CATO. Let me see.

He looks under YOUTH's *blanket.*

Oh. Let's get you up there.

He lifts YOUTH *onto the bench.*

Easy . . . lean on me. Careful. Don't put any weight on that now. There you are. Rest it. Do you want some wine?

YOUTH. Yes. Thank you.

CATO *pours some, offers it to* YOUTH, *who is able to hold it.*

Pause.

CATO. Is this your place?

YOUTH. No.

CATO. I was told to come here. Were you looting? Did someone catch you looting and teach you a lesson?

YOUTH. No.

CATO. Good. I've a very poor opinion of looters. A very selfish approach to war. If you were a looter I'd say you got just what you deserved. Teach you a lesson. You'd not loot again. Hmm . . . Have you any experience of agricultural work?

YOUTH. What?

CATO. Someone's slashed into your hamstring. Usually that's what happens to slaves, if they're not to be sent to work in the fields. You're not dressed as a slave, you don't look like a slave, and yet someone has recently decided that you are a slave. And they don't want you leaving for a while. That's my reading of the situation. What are you doing here?

YOUTH. I was taken here.

CATO. By a man called Gregor?

YOUTH. Yes. Gregor.

CATO. Did he do this?

YOUTH. No.

CATO. Good. I'm glad. There are many things about Gregor I don't like, but violence isn't one of them.

CATO *fetches a white sheet and starts ripping it to form bandages. As he speaks, he bandages* YOUTH's *calf, tenderly and professionally.*

I'm no first-aider. These days I break a nail and a doctor takes care of it for me. So this might not be doing much good. It'll give the wound a bit of protection until someone else can have a look at it. (*Pause.*) Though to be honest, I don't know who that might be.

YOUTH. My people will look after me.

CATO. Of course, of course. You've been through a lot. (*Pause*.) Tell me. Why did Gregor bring you here?

YOUTH. To be . . . to be his secretary.

CATO. I see. Did he . . . did he hurt you in any way?

YOUTH. No. Not him. The other one.

CATO. Who was the other one?

YOUTH. I don't know.

CATO. Did either of them . . . did Gregor make advances towards you that seemed . . . unusual.

YOUTH. No. Not really.

CATO. 'Not really.' A bit, then. Hmm. You're here of your own free will?

YOUTH. I'm a hostage.

CATO. Gregor took you as a hostage? Against who?

YOUTH *rolls his head again*.

Here, have some more wine. You can tell me everything. Trust me.

YOUTH. There were three hundred of us.

CATO. One of those hostages? What are you doing here? You should have been sent to Utica.

YOUTH. Gregor chose me. He . . . he liked my face.

CATO. You do have . . . beautiful features. Not at their best right now, but I can tell . . .

YOUTH. He needed a secretary.

CATO. No, he didn't. He needed company. And he did you no favours. The others were released. Your leaders gave up your armoury, we released our hostages. Then they double-crossed us.

YOUTH. You mean they fought.

CATO. Exactly. Which I suppose makes you a hostage who's not been redeemed. (*Pause*.) Is Gregor coming back for you?

YOUTH. No.

CATO. You're a poor liar. Often the sign of a good man. I'll wait for a while. Gregor and I have some catching up to do.

YOUTH *makes a pained noise*.

Are you OK?

YOUTH. It's just . . . my leg.

CATO. Listen . . . It must be extremely painful. You're young and noble, so probably you haven't experienced much pain like this before. But crying isn't going to make it any better and it shows weakness. You're at that age where you can choose. Are you going to face this like a boy or like a man?

YOUTH. It hurts.

CATO. At the moment I'm in a very bad mood with your countrymen. They've succeeded in turning a very simple operation into a war. And wars bring expenses. I hate expenses. And to what end? The result is the same. Carthage is destroyed. Their homes are destroyed. Now most families will be missing a son or a husband because they'd rather stay, fight and die than leave the town. I hate that . . . It's a waste of resources – yours and mine. They've let their emotions get the better of them. But I will say one thing. They were brave. Foolishly brave, perhaps, but brave nonetheless. So think about that when your leg hurts and your first reaction is to blub like a baby.

YOUTH. I am trying.

CATO. Good. Keep trying, only harder. And bear in mind that when the first Roman soldier was killed, any hostages became forfeit. I didn't know we had any, but now I find that we do I'm almost duty bound to kill you.

YOUTH. Who are you?

CATO. All you need to know is that this is my war. And you're in it.

YOUTH. I don't fear death.

CATO. Then you're a fool. If all you lot feared death a bit
more, this whole business would have been a lot cheaper all
round.

GREGOR *enters*.

GREGOR. Cato!

CATO. Ah, good evening, Gregor. That wasn't a hand twitching
towards a dagger was it?

GREGOR. No . . . not at all.

CATO. I was sure I saw a twitch.

GREGOR. No . . . maybe a twitch. I couldn't be sure it was
you.

CATO. Because if you do want to draw your dagger on me,
now would be the time to do it. There won't be another
chance after this. This is the last time you and me will be
alone together. (*Glances at* YOUTH.) Or almost alone.

GREGOR. I've no wish, no wish at all to threaten you. I'm
just nervous. It's dangerous out there. Buildings on fire . . .
gangs . . . and I think . . . I think I was followed.

CATO. Why didn't you make sure?

YOUTH. My family?

CATO. Be quiet, you.

GREGOR. It's all right, Cato. I . . . I found out where your
family are.

CATO. Don't tell me what's all right and what's not all right.
You've completely forgotten why you're here.

GREGOR. No. No, I haven't.

CATO. Why are you here, then? Answer me. Why are you
here?

GREGOR. To . . . to serve Rome. To do Rome's will.

CATO. Yes. And that's my will. You're here to do what I say.
Did I treat you unfairly, Gregor? What injury did I do you?
Cato's man in Carthage, regular reports on the generals and
some clean-up work. My eyes and ears, then back to Rome

for a fresh start. Was that such a bad punishment for what
you did? So bad that you neglect your duties? So bad that
you only leave your little sanctuary here to find his family?
He is more important than me? Is that the message here?

GREGOR. No. I've been ill. That's why things haven't gone
well. Very ill. A fever. I've been feeling better today. That's
why I went out. To see if I could help. I said to the boy here
I'd keep an eye out, that's all. I felt sorry for him.

YOUTH. Where are they?

GREGOR. Not now, Youth.

CATO. Please don't take me for a fool. On top of everything
else. Not that. I didn't travel from Rome, waste my time
and money making peace deals with the forts, then walk
through this burning cesspool of a city to hear you taking
me for a fool. You went out to find his family. The captor
waiting on the hostage. You think you're in love with him –
the old weakness. And all the time you're keeping him
happy, not a word to me. Not a word. If I can learn anything
from this – and one must try – it's that mercy is an overrated
virtue.

GREGOR. What do you mean?

CATO. I mean I could have saved Rome a lot of money and
myself a lot of time by having you killed in Rome. Well,
tell him where his family is. If first impressions count, he's
worth ten of you.

YOUTH. Are they alive?

GREGOR. I think so. They're in the temple. It's not been
taken yet. Everyone in the forts is either dead or a prisoner.

YOUTH. He said he made peace deals.

GREGOR. It wasn't . . . Rome's finest moment. But your
family are brave. They've not surrendered. There's a lot of
them in there. They must know it's hopeless, but they won't
come out.

CATO. That expensive Carthaginian bravery again. You can be
proud.

YOUTH. I am. Now I can die.

GREGOR. I promised to rescue them. It was impossible.

YOUTH. I never expected it.

GREGOR. But I found them. And I came back.

YOUTH. Thank you.

CATO. This is very touching. So are the forts all taken?

GREGOR. If I could have got them out, I would have.

YOUTH. It was impossible.

GREGOR. Yes . . . impossible.

CATO *cuffs* GREGOR *round the head.*

CATO. Senator. A reminder. Me – Cato. Him – a hostage. No, not even a hostage. A slave, if he's lucky. Get your priorities right. Are the forts all taken?

GREGOR. All of them. The temple's all that's left, but there's people hiding in houses, ready to attack. The fires are spreading. We shouldn't stay here too long.

CATO. Our soldiers know what they're doing. Now. We're safe enough.

GREGOR. It's not just Romans doing the damage. The Carthaginians as well. Destroying anything that might be useful to us.

CATO. All of a sudden it's 'us' again. I thought you'd switched sides.

GREGOR. No. Never.

CATO. Or was it that you were above war? Too unaesthetic for a man of your tastes?

GREGOR. No . . . I was ill.

CATO. You were drinking. Moping around.

GREGOR. I'll make it up to you. But we'd better leave. I think I was followed. If they knew a Roman consul was staying here . . .

CATO. They'd send us up in flames. (*To* YOUTH.) Does that bother you?

YOUTH. If I have no city, no family . . . no. It doesn't bother me.

CATO. There will be rebuilding. A lot of lucrative contracts. You'd be working for us but . . . there's always winners and losers in war. On both sides.

YOUTH. I won't work for you.

CATO (*looking to the west*). It's a shame you can't stand up. Can't see the smoke and fire of a dying city. It might give you some sort of closure – give you the shock you need to face up to the realities of the situation . . . let you reassess your options. For my part, I find it an almost . . . overwhelming view. A setting sun, bright orange round dark clouds, and the rising smog of the death of Carthage. It's . . . it's a very moving moment. However, you must suit yourself.

MARCUS *enters – bloody from a head wound.*

MARCUS. Cato.

CATO. Marcus . . . what happened?

MARCUS. A stone. In the centre, no one notices you. It's just fire and noise. People screaming, buildings falling. No one has time to stop and see you. They're rescuing possessions, or family . . . heading for the country.

CATO. They should have done that in the beginning.

MARCUS. But the further from the city, the more dangerous it is. Looters, gangs, even children throwing things. We should go.

CATO. This isn't a popularity contest. It's inevitable people will resist. Send the order – after the main city's gone, spread to the outskirts. Level the whole place. Don't leave a house standing.

MARCUS. I saw you out there, Gregor. Skulking around.

GREGOR. Seeing what I could do. To help.

MARCUS. Very little, I imagine.

CATO. Don't underestimate Gregor. When he wants to be, he can be very effective. It's just that Rome's will isn't enough. It takes a young lad with good skin and an absent father to motivate our senator friend.

MARCUS (*smiles at* YOUTH). How's your leg?

YOUTH. One of them's fine.

MARCUS. Insolent little prick.

CATO. Calm, calm. I had an idea that might be your handiwork. I was going to accuse you of being a little overzealous.

MARCUS (*shrugs*). It's what we do to slaves.

CATO. A fit young man is a resource, Marcus. To be used. Try to think before you cripple them. This fellow could have been working on your estate.

MARCUS. I don't have an estate.

CATO. Not yet, not yet. Anyway, it doesn't matter. You made a call. A hamstrung Carthaginian hostage isn't high on my list of priorities right now. And given that his family seem to be locked in a temple, there doesn't seem to be any point hanging on to him.

MARCUS. The temple's gone.

GREGOR. What do you mean, gone?

MARCUS. Up in flames. Everyone dead.

GREGOR. So now we set fire to temples . . .

MARCUS. No. We tried, but it was solid stone. We couldn't. They did. From inside.

CATO (*to* YOUTH). You seem unmoved.

YOUTH. I knew it. I knew they would never belong to Rome.

CATO. You can't be pleased they died screaming.

MARCUS. That's the thing. With the forts and other buildings on fire, all you could hear across the city was screaming. Not screams of fear, or even pain. It was like one big scream of a city dying. I . . . I hadn't heard anything like it before. But when the temple was on fire, it was silent. Just the noise of the flames, and the building collapsing. No screams. And the thing is, it wasn't just Carthaginians in there. There were Roman deserters as well. Where did their courage come from?

CATO. Possibly the thought of what awaited them. More likely they all died of smoke inhalation before the fire took hold. I've seen a lot of things in my lifetime, but I've never seen a man burn to death without screaming.

GREGOR *goes to* YOUTH *and strokes his cheek.*

GREGOR. I'm sorry.

YOUTH. Get your hand off me.

GREGOR. You're upset.

YOUTH. If you hadn't decided you liked my face, I would have been released. You didn't tell me that.

GREGOR. I . . . I didn't know.

YOUTH. I could have died with my family. Instead of here.

GREGOR. You're not going to die. Your leg . . . you'll still be able to move. I'll help you.

CATO. The young fellow's a step ahead of you. He knows his leg's not going to kill him. You are.

GREGOR. No, Cato. There's no need. Why?

CATO. Because he's a hostage. And because he's Carthage. He has the spirit and pride of his city. His family lie charred and there's no mourning in his eyes. Just vengeance. He is Carthage, and Carthage must be destroyed.

GREGOR. I can't do it.

CATO. Marcus, who did you say was in the temple? Brave Carthaginians and . . . who else?

MARCUS. Deserters.

CATO. Deserters. That was it. Well, it looks like we've got our own little temple going on right here. One brave Carthaginian and a general refusing a direct order. In my eyes, that's desertion. What do we know happens to deserters? Any ideas? Nothing? Marcus?

MARCUS. They die.

GREGOR. But I couldn't. Any other order, Cato. I can still be a friend to you.

CATO. You idiot. You think friendship's possible now. Gregor, I'm giving you one last chance. Your desertion started when you gave up doing your job, shacked up with a hostage and went on the booze. I don't need to do this. I could kill you in good conscience right now. But if you can do this . . . maybe I can start thinking of a way back for you.

GREGOR. Anything else . . .

CATO. He's going to die, fool. Either with you or without you. Show me your dagger.

GREGOR *does so.*

Hand it over.

GREGOR *does so.*

You have something in you, Gregor, that you can't control. I'm giving you the chance to deal with that. Look at his face. That's the face you're going to see every time you're in the bath, or the gym, when you get back to Rome. That's the face that's going to keep you pure.

Pause. CATO *gives* GREGOR *the dagger back.*

It's a sharp blade. You can kill him quickly. Stand up, lad.

YOUTH *stands up, leaning on the bench.*

Do it.

GREGOR *is still, holding the dagger and facing* YOUTH. CATO *and* MARCUS *back off.*

GREGOR (*after a long pause, very quietly*). If I was to stick this in you, Youth, you wouldn't feel a thing. Youth . . . I'm so sorry.

With a roar, GREGOR *charges* CATO. CATO *is ready, sidesteps, and sticks a knife into* GREGOR's *stomach.* GREGOR *collapses, blood coming from his stomach.* MARCUS *is in there quickly, ready for the kill.*

CATO. It's all right, Marcus.

MARCUS. You sure . . . You all right?

CATO. Yes . . . a little weary. I hate wasting my time. Get the
rope and tie them both up.

MARCUS. Together?

CATO. Why not? Oh, stop moaning, Gregor. You've enough
extra flesh there to cope with a knife. I just flicked you.

As CATO *speaks,* MARCUS *ties* YOUTH *and then*
GREGOR *to a pillar.* CATO *sits, mops his brow, tired.*

You understand all about chain of command. That was never
a confusion for you. But you have no idea about chain of
responsibility. If you tell enough people that Carthage must
be destroyed, then Carthage will be destroyed. You thought
you could just hide in your bath while a city was razed to
the ground. But no . . . I wanted you to see it. But you
couldn't. Couldn't face it. Just tried to create your own little
Rome in Carthage. But what was Rome for you? Booze,
boys and politics. Seems like you found two out of three. But
you gave up too easily on the only important one. Politics
matters. Booze and boys . . . they're for now. Politics is for
the future. Politics means action. Actions have consequences.
Everything you couldn't handle here was started by you.
And me. And Marcus. Face it, Gregor. You're responsible.

You represent waste. Someone who could have made a
contribution but didn't. You let your weaknesses rule you.

David was off limits, as simple as that. A man who controls
his weaknesses acknowledges that – gets himself a slave,
or a prostitute. I condemn that man, but such is the way of
things at the moment. But David was freeborn. I gave you a
chance, to face up to things, to see a strategy through. But
you're weak. A hostage tempts you to ignore the chaos all
around you. You're waste. You're no use.

Do you think you're in love when you do these things? Do
you think there's a place for that kind of love, for any kind
of love? In war?

You can't be trusted in a trial. You know too much. So I, Cato, find you guilty of desertion. Your wife and children will be looked after; I have no mean streak. But your estate will be forfeit. I'm giving it to Marcus.

MARCUS *looks surprised.*

No, Marcus, you deserve it. Perhaps there'll be a lesson for others there.

CATO *gets up.*

I feel I should say I'm sorry about this, but I'm not. I've spent the day briefing generals, negotiating with the enemy, supervising fire, destruction and death. Getting things done. This is trivial. A tidying up. Tomorrow, I've got to organise an occupation, rebuild morale, run the fucking Republic. I shouldn't be wasting time on this. We'll start the fire downstairs. There's no wind; hopefully the smoke'll get you first. But perhaps the roof will collapse and you'll fall into a burning building. It's hard to know.

He touches YOUTH*'s head, the slightest of caresses.*

I could kill you quickly now, lad, if you want, but I want you to imagine you're in the temple. With your family. Do that for me.

Come on, Marcus.

CATO *and* MARCUS *exit.*

GREGOR*'s hands almost reach* YOUTH*'s around the pillar.*

GREGOR. Hold my hand, Youth. Reach for it.

Silence.

Youth . . . Hannibal. Let us hold hands. Do you want to die alone?

YOUTH. I'm not alone.

Smoke rises from the floor.

Lights out.

The End.

A Nick Hern Book

Carthage Must Be Destroyed first published in Great Britain as a paperback original in 2007 by Nick Hern Books Limited, 14 Larden Road, London W3 7ST in association with the Traverse Theatre, Edinburgh

Carthage Must Be Destroyed copyright © 2007 Alan Wilkins

Alan Wilkins has asserted his right to be identified as the author of this work

Cover image: Laurence Winram with special thanks to the National Galleries of Scotland

Cover design: Ned Hoste, 2H

Typeset by Country Setting, Kingsdown, Kent CT14 8ES
Printed in Great Britain by Biddles, King's Lynn

A CIP catalogue record for this book is available from the British Library

ISBN 978 1 85459 985 8